Removing Anti-Judaism from the Pulpit

Removing Anti-Judaism from the Pulpit

Editors
Howard Clark Kee
Irvin J. Borowsky

American Interfaith Institute • Philadelphia
Continuum • New York

1996
The Continuum Publishing Company
370 Lexington Avenue
New York, NY 10017

Printed in the United States of America

Library of Congress Cataloging-in-Publication Data

Removing anti-Judaism from the pulpit / editors, Howard Clark
   Kee, Irvin J. Borowsky.
      p. cm.
   Includes bibliographical references and index.
   ISBN 0-8264-0927-X
   1. Judaism (Christian theology) 2. Christianity and antisemitism.
3. Preaching. I. Kee, Howard Clark. II. Borowsky, Irvin J.
BT93.R45 1996
261.2'6—dc20   96-22918
                                                                      CIP

Contents

FOREWORD

The Language of Religion:
A Force for Asserting Life;
A Force for Degradation

Irvin J. Borowsky

The language of the Bible is powerful, especially when presented in a beautifully bound edition. And when the same words are spoken from the pulpit, their influence is magnified countless times. Over the centuries, they have created a vision for millions of Christians by giving form to religious concepts that elevate their own existence within life. But, tragically, some of these words have also brought havoc, torture, and death to millions of Jews. This was not the intention of the righteous people who authored the texts of the Bible in order to proclaim and solidify the love Jesus taught.

Language has a spirit all its own, a capricious quality all its own—a capricious quality that is recognized by truth-seekers as an entity in flux, the mirror of a society in time, the sensitive barometer of an era. In the hands of manipulators, however, words can be skewed to produce poisonous falsehoods and become major weapons. These words in Christian literature and liturgy taken out of context have been exploited by bigots in order to foster prejudice and distrust of the Jewish people.

As a result, millions of Jews in Europe have been harassed, been forced to leave their homelands, and been murdered when the derogatory references about Jews in the New Testament were exploited by purveyors of hate.

In these references, all Jewry is spoken of as one, and, collectively, they are blamed for the death of Jesus. Jews from ancient times to the present are damned in prose that virulently defames and decries all Jews. Surely it is a paradox that the references set the stage for hostility and murder of those whose heritage and roots were from the same family tree as that of Jesus.

Curiously, these passages ignore the Jewishness of Mary and Joseph. Indeed, Mary is actually presented as having been born into the Christian faith. Her Jewish roots are completely omitted.

It is doubtful that many European Christians would have assisted in the murder of a million-and-a-half Jewish children just fifty years ago if they had been aware that the Mother of Jesus was as Jewish as the parents of those innocent children.

In most editions of the New Testament, the Jews are presented as "the people who killed Jesus;" a people to be despised for all eternity. It is this portrait that is the genesis of the anti-Jewish poison that has been passed down from generation to generation.

Over the past eight centuries, one out of every two Jews was murdered in Europe. There are now fewer than fourteen million survivors left in the entire world. The vigor of Judaism in the first century which permitted the flowering of new thought, new directions, new concepts, has been denigrated, denied, and exploited over and over by bigoted and ambitious dictators.

Portions of Christian literature may be held responsible for the murder-producing speeches of Hitler and his associates. The Nazis would not have succeeded in disseminating their brand of racist anti-Semitism had they not been confident of the pervasive, durable hatred of Jews; a hatred rooted in some of the language of the New Testament. Hitler never personally murdered Jews, but millions participated in this madness which was so alien to true Christian principles.

Today, there are approximately seven thousand different editions of the New Testament in print. Although they vary, each claims to be an accurate interpretation of the ancient Greek text. The one shared element is that all versions slander the Jews, thereby insuring continuation of a bottomless tradition of hatred.

Even more inflammatory are some of the current "children's Bibles" which are uneven interpretations from a variety of New Testament editions. They contain fearful passages that teach Christian children, at the most impressionable time of their lives, to distrust and hate Jews. They serve to perpetuate and exacerbate still further hostile feelings against Jews. Nor is the young reader or recent convert to Christianity given any inclination that all the founders of Christianity were Jewish: Jesus, John the Baptist, Paul, Matthew, and the Apostles, or that their message was not intended to promote hatred of their own people.

Today, countless Christian scholars and theologians have come to terms with the importance of language as a central element in religious concept and practice. They recognize that the contemporary Jewish people are survivors of a hatred that is based on words that deny the reality of historical truths of the first century.

Key participants in the work of the American Interfaith Institute are a worldwide network of Christian theologians who are committed to redefining the anti-Jewish statements found in the Scriptures. Because they know that both Christianity and rabbinic Judaism have evolved from ancient Hebrew sources, these scholars are actively engaged in the process of studying and rethinking Jewish-Christian relationships and advocating new perceptions that will replace old distortions. Sadly, many passages still charge Jews with Jesus' death. Here are examples:

John 5:16 *And therefore did the Jews persecute Jesus, and sought to slay him, because he had done these things on the Sabbath day.*

John 7:1 *After these things Jesus walked in Galilee; for he would not walk in Judea, because the Jews sought to kill him.*

Acts 9:23 *And after that many days were fulfilled, the Jews took counsel to kill him.*

Christians who have no hatred of the Jewish people respond that these passages relate only to a specific historical situation of two thousand years ago, and are not intended to teach hatred. Yet, in a series of academic seminars, when the words "Jesus" and "Mohammed" were exchanged in the above passages and "Jew" and "Christian" were also exchanged, the responses of the participants were sensitive and supportive. Using this exchange, John 7:1 would read:

After these things Mohammed walked in Galilee for he would not walk in Judea, because the Christians sought to slay him.

How safe would a Christian be, living in a Moslem country, if statements like the above appeared in the Koran and were quoted freely by preachers of Islam?

But progress is being made. We are pleased to report many advances in recent years in the area of New Testament research, translation, and clarification. The American Bible Society, Oxford University Press, and several publishers of children's bibles have followed our recommendations and removed much of the anti-Jewish tenor from their newest editions.

Extraordinary progress is being made from the pulpit. The chapters appearing in this book reflect the work of Christian scholars and theologians who are dedicated to accurate and nonaccusatory preaching; to incorporating truth and authenticity into the language of their faith. Clearly, the Jewish founders of Christianity would support these clarifications in order to break the cycle of violence against Jews for all time.

Future generations of Jews and Christians will not be divided by a collective memory of hate and fear but, instead, will be united in a shared vision of heritage, freedom, and love.

It is this insight, now so well accepted and widely advocated by enlightened theologians and scholars worldwide, that will influence and expand Jewish–Christian relationships everywhere; that will give new strength to the language of religion as a force for asserting life.

Contributors and Participants

Hugh Anderson
Professor of New Testament Emeritus
Faculty of Divinity
University of Edinburgh, Scotland

Ronald J. Allen
Assistant Professor of
  New Testament and Preaching
Christian Theological Seminary
Indianapolis, Indiana

Wallace M. Alston, Jr.
Senior Minister
  Nassau Presbyterian Church
Princeton, New Jersey

Irvin J. Borowsky
Chairman
American Interfaith Institute
  Living History Museum
  World Alliance of Interfaith
  Organizations
Philadelphia, Pennsylvania

Harry James Cargas
Department of Religion
  Webster University
St. Louis, Missouri

Robert J. Daly, S.J.
Jesuit Priest and Professor of Theology
Boston College
Editor of *Theological Studies*
Chestnut Hill, Massachusetts

Stanley Hauerwas
Gilbert T. Rowe Professor of
  Theological Ethics
The Divinity School
Duke University
Durham, North Carolina

Frederick D. Holmgren
Research Professor of Old Testament
North Park Theological Seminary
Chicago, Illinois

Howard Clark Kee
Professor Biblical Studies, Emeritus
Boston University
Philadelphia, Pennsylvania

Nancy M. Malone, O.S.U.
Co-Editor of *Cross Currents*
  The Journal of the Association for
  Religion and Intellectual Life
College of New Rochelle
New Rochelle, New York

Martin E. Marty
The Fairfax M. Cone Distinguished
  Service Professor of the History
  of Modern Christianity
Editor of *Christian Century*
University of Chicago, Chicago, Illinois

Carol Ann Morrow
Assistant Editor
  St. Anthony Messenger
Cincinnati, Ohio

John T. Pawlikowski, O.S.M., Ph.D.
Professor Catholic Theological Union
  of Social Ethics
Chicago, Illlinois

Peter C. Phan
Professor and Chair
  School of Religious Studies Department
  of Theology
Catholic University of America
Washington, District of Columbia

David H. C. Read
Minister Emeritus, Madison Avenue
  Presbyterian Church
Editor of *The Living Pulpit*
New York, New York

Clark M. Williamson
Indiana Chair of Christian Thought
Christian Theological Seminary
Indianapolis, Indiana

William H. Willimon
Dean of the Chapel and
  Professor of Christian Ministry
Duke University Chapel
Durham, North Carolina

ABBREVIATIONS

Publications:
JBL — Journal of Biblical Literature
NEB —New English Bible
RSV — Revised Standard Version

Publishing Agencies:
ADL — Anti-Defamation League
NCCB — National Conference of Catholic Bishops
WCC — World Council of Churches

Biblical Books:
Abbreviations follow standard form of *Chicago Manual of Style*, with variations according to whether the text cited is from Protestant, Catholic, or Jewish versions of the Scriptures.

Roman Catholic Orders:
S.J. — Society of Jesus
O.F.M. — Order of Friars Minor
O.S.M. — Order of Servite Fathers

INTRODUCTION

Gaining New Perspectives on the Relationships between Judaism and Christianity

Howard Clark Kee

This is the year in which we recall with sorrow and revulsion the Holocaust, which came to international attention fifty years ago. Although intellectual, historical, and political developments in the latter half of the current century have enabled those who stand within two of the great monotheistic traditions—Judaism and Christianity—to gain new understanding of the common features in these religious movements, and thereby to shed new light on the differences, tensions still persist between adherents of each of them. We stand at a time when interreligious conflicts are mounting across the world, while bigotry is capturing the minds of young people in many places. This is the basic factor in the fighting that has arisen in the former Yugoslavia between Muslims, Orthodox, and Catholic Christians. It is a major impediment to peace in the Middle East, and is giving rise to mounting tensions between Christian and Muslim Blacks in the United States. At a time when increased understanding and acceptance of religious differences are imperative there are two important kinds of development which have the potential to provide new information and insights and thereby to foster mutual acceptance between Jews and Christians.

Among the most important historical developments have been (1) the discovery of ancient Jewish and Christian documents, many of them previously unknown, and (2) the emergence of fresh analyses of ancient Jewish sources and traditions which have resulted in new understandings of the evolution of Judaism in the post-exilic period and of the separate paths taken by Jews and Christians from the first century onward. Awareness of this new evidence and the growing sensitivity of scholars and leaders in these two traditions to the tensions and misconceptions that have arisen over the centuries between Jews and Christians require fresh analyses of this recently recovered information, as well as a broad-based effort to convey the results of these finds to a wider readership than that of the field of technical scholarship alone. An important feature of the need and opportunity for increased understanding of these religious traditions is the widespread effort toward fresh translations of early Christian writings. These should reflect accurately the complex situations which existed among those who by the second century C.E. came to be sharply differentiated as Jews and Christians. What must be avoided is reading later perceptions of these movements by their respective membership back into the crucial first century of their development.

Although there is evidence in the popular media of widespread interest in such items as the Dead Sea Scrolls and the historical Jesus, there has been far too little attention given to the new perspectives in which the origins of Christianity and the emergence of rabbinic Judaism must now be seen. There have been encouraging developments among Bible publishers, who are now broadly committed to reworking the translations to remove the implicit claims that the whole of the Jewish people were involved in and took responsibility for the death of Jesus. But it is essential that sensitivity be raised among preachers and teachers in the Christian communities on these issues, and that information be provided to correct the historical misconceptions on which anti-Judaism has been based.

The essays which follow in this volume are of two types: (1) those in the first section which address the historical and interpretive issues and assumptions which have fostered anti-Judaism; and (2) examples of sermons which address this issue. They have been prepared by a distinguished group of Catholic and Protestant scholars and clergy. The aim of both types is to heighten sensitivity to the issue of anti-Judaism in Christian pulpits, and to increase both knowledge of the evidence about Christian origins and fresh approaches which will foster mutual understanding between Jews and Christians.

SECTION ONE

CHAPTER ONE

Removing Anti-Judaism from the Christian Pulpit

Martin E. Marty

Christians, be they Orthodox, Roman Catholic, or Protestant all value preaching. They cite Paul the Apostle who argued that faith comes by hearing, and hearing by the word of God, a word that demands preaching and preachers. While Orthodox and Roman Catholic worshipers usually gather before the altar or around the table for the Eucharist, Protestants, most of whom also value the sacred meal, more likely make the pulpit their focus. So "pulpit" has come to represent the place and the act where faith is to be engendered with conversion following; where the messages of judgment and grace issue forth; where nurture and education are supported; where hearers are to get guidance and inspiration for their lives.

No instrument is more important for reaching and forming the opinions of adults in congregations than is the pulpit. The homilies or sermons issuing from it may be of varying degrees of quality and styles, but the intention remains to make the act of disseminating the oral word in formal circumstances the central act of worship, no doubt the central act of communication, in much of Christianity.

While some preaching is topical and, in liberal Protestant pulpits, may take on lecture form, most Christian preaching takes off from a biblical text and relates it to the contemporary scene and the lives of those who hear. The text may be from the Hebrew Scriptures or the New Testament; two out of four texts read each week in liturgical services that employ a lectionary are from the New Testament, and one might well surmise that while there are many expositions of what most Christians call the Old Testament, the New Testament inspires more preaching than not.

The New Testament, whether in the four Gospels or, from further back in the book and in most cases from further back in time, in the collection of letters and treatises called the Epistles, very often includes texts that reveal the earliest Christian communities being busy drawing boundaries. The texts suggest varying degrees of relation to the synagogue in which Jewish Christianity was defined or to Judaism, with which Gentile Christianity was wrestling. The drama of defining and separating creates problems for preachers and audiences twenty centuries later.

Most if not all religions are born critical of their antecedents and environs. If they concurred with what went before or simply accepted what was around, new faiths or religions or traditions, call them what one will, would not have been needed. They would not have found a niche or been regarded as credible. Insofar as these faiths were transmitted through communication for which we have textual evidence, it is clear that their texts often contained demeaning if not devastating reference to the different, the other. Because that "other" is rarely represented by a vital faith, today one might say in such cases, "No Offense." Thus New Testament writers contended against the religions of Greece and Rome as represented wherever the young church would go, but these ancient cults have few organized, explicit followings today. The Hebrew Scriptures have hundreds of horrifying references to Canaanite, Egyptian, Babylonian, and other faiths who have no perceived surviving derivative communities. No harm done, therefore, when one quotes a prophet attacking them.

The case of Christian denunciations of Judaism, however, is different. The preacher may say that the Romans and the Jews killed Jesus, the originating and central figure in Christianity, and often called "the Son of God." The listener does not associate the Italian down the block with the lineage of Pontius Pilate and the others in the Roman cast of characters. But she may associate ancient Jews with the contemporary Jews next door. At least, Christians have done so for many centuries, with lethal consequences. The old pictures get reinforced when the scriptural references get transferred and applied or misapplied to

Jews, who have been spiritual cousins and yet victims through the centuries of Christians, who got much of their plot from what they heard in sermons.

Hence there are good reasons to attack the issue of anti-Judaism in the pulpit. That may not be the only plausible place to start. Constructive efforts have been made with much success to reform the literature for the education of children across the denominational spectrum with positive effect. Opinion polls show an impressively high degree of Christian tolerance of and respect for Jews and Judaism. Statistically, anti-Judaism is hardly significant. It is not respectable to be intolerant, and whenever the polltaker is on the phone or at the door, "Come to think of it," one says, "there are no reasons that come to mind to express anti-Jewish attitudes." Governmental policy in the United States protects all faiths, not least of all Judaism. Still, the Christian congregations can be agents of conflict in local communities, and what is said from the pulpit can and will have consequences in the hearing and lives of citizens.

Attempts to "remove anti-Judaism from the pulpit," therefore, are crucial to the sustaining and further development of promising Christian–Jewish relations. While not possessing a sunny view of human nature or an optimistic philosophy of history, I am going to posit general good will on the part of most of the faithful. There exists, of course, some organized and pathological anti-Semitism, which demands its separate analysis. Here the concern is with the majority of circumstances, where ordinary people of ordinary good will who want to do the right thing gather. They do not come to get signals on how to desecrate synagogues, drive out the Jews, assert that there was no Holocaust, oppose Israel, or say insulting things to or about their neighbor. I have reasonably alert ears and a record of virtually weekly church attendance every Sunday for two thirds of a century, in many congregations of many denominations in many parts of the world. I would be hard pressed to recall a single sermon in which anything of that sort was an aim or memorable element.

On the other hand, with most other active Christians, I know I have been through the biblical text of the church year(s) many times, and heard few expositions of the anti-Jewish references in the texts, at least references that helped the congregation cope with the theological and practical ways of relating to the different, the other—who is a Jew, or that is Judaism. Unexpounded, unexplained, or mistreated, these texts can work ill effect at the expense to the integrity of Judaism and Christian faith and community alike. In what follows I will set forth, as briefly as possible, given the limits of space for each chapter in this book, some assertions designed to explain the situation of the pulpit and then to make some suggestions about interpreting what goes on in and from it and what to do about it.

The New Testament has reference to being a "fool for Christ." Protestant theologian Reinhold Niebuhr once said that there was a difference between being a fool for Christ and a damn fool. We must let readers decide which I am, for accepting the assignment in which the second half of this chapter will be a sermon that I preached, something I regard as an example, though it may not come to be regarded as exemplary. Here, then, are some preliminary notices, theses, and suggestions:

1. There is no such a thing as the "the pulpit." What goes on in a Unitarian Universalist sanctuary differs more than mildly from the act and expectations of preaching in a fundamentalist Protestant congregation. Each has to examine its own preaching tradition, concepts of how to use texts, and the circumstances if they want to "go deep" in dealing with this issue.

2. There are few external controls on most pulpits. It is extremely rare for ecclesiastical authority and almost nonexistent as a possibility that in the ordinary run of things efforts can be made "from on top" to control the message. Local circumstances, fear of crowds or crowd pleasing, and the like, have some effect. But essentially the pulpit is free, and good behavior in it has to be a matter of persuasion and not coercion, of education and not control.

3. The when and where of the pulpit matters. In the United States it may be hard for most Jews to realize that what we are taking up here is not seen as urgent in most places where there are Christian pulpits. Thus: there are fewer Jews *in the whole world* than there are members of the Southern Baptist Convention, most of them in the South, in the United States alone. Some population experts say that two-thirds of American Jews live within one hundred miles of New York.

Not many Protestants, at least not many white Protestants do. This does not mean that anti-Judaism is not expressed in town and country, small city, and other churches. It means that one cannot assume the same measures of sensitivity or the same prospects for damage in all places.

4. No matter what is done, anti-Judaism will not satisfyingly be "removed" from all preaching, all pulpits. All religions offend, all preaching is offensive; that is, if religion or preaching is provocative, it will be found to be dealing ambiguously with complex textual traditions, flawed human instruments in the pulpit, and great diversity in the pew. Most preachers will not have a Ph.D. in Jewish–Christian Relations studies, and a shockingly large number of them will not be where there are clear existential and practical reasons to make the revisioning of textual sermon traditions urgent or even a frequently noticed priority. It is very difficult to handle anti-Judaic features in texts that mainly promote other themes. The sermon I append illustrates that. It was originally preached at a jazz Mass during a jazz festival at a downtown loft-church; I removed those jazzy references and kept mainly those parts that dealt with problematic anti-Judaic ("scribes and Pharisees") parts of the text. But when all is done and said, or preached, there will have to be a reckoning with the fact that, given several hundred thousand pulpits in use each week, not everything will go right. Making more things go right is the goal of efforts like this book.

5. To be a bit more controversial: the way to remove anti-Judaic elements from preaching is *not* to produce an expurgated Bible. When groups like the Music of the Baroque in Chicago sing the *St. John Passion* of Bach, as an example, I sometimes am asked to annotate the program notes. Many of the singers, sponsors, and audience members are Jews. Read the text of the *St. John Passion* with Jews in mind and you will find good reason to be tempted to expurgate it, or to sing something else. Yet I have read that the *Passion* is heard in Israel as the music of Richard Wagner, a modern anti-Semite, is not. Bach's music, we are told, belongs to the common patrimony [matrimony?] of Jews and Christians, their cultural heritage. He has to be confronted, enjoyed, wrestled with, and annotated. As an annotator I keep coming back to the scary awareness that if one really took out eraser or purging

machine and started editing, there would be little of that
Gospel text left to sing. Better to annotate, and then rely on the
sophistication of hearers.

6. To expect all Christian preaching to be nonsupersessionist,
that is, to insist that Judaism remains a faith community with
its own integrity; that it is not simply a relic of Act I of a two-
act drama in which it has no meaning or say; that Christianity
is not a superior faith in the pop-Enlightenment sense of "my
religion is better than yours"; that there be an elder sibling and
younger sibling relation between the faiths in every sermon is
unrealistic. Most preachers do not go to elite interdenomina-
tional, interfaith theological schools. Though many are products of fine seminaries, stocked with first-rate biblical scholars
and teachers of preaching, most have not had on their agenda
the task of thinking through all the theological assumptions
behind antisupersessionism.

What is more, there would probably be a rise in anti-Judaism
and anti-elite Christianism if efforts were made to push the
supersessionist agenda. Most Christians have a simple faith in
simple stories. Like most people of faith, they are locked into
subcommunities that dig in, no matter what the scholars have
to say. They have their lives to live and don't create for themselves enlarged problems where they experience problems
hardly at all. They would not know Anselm's substitutionary
theory of the atonement from Ritschlian moral influence theory. They may be college graduates, but on this theme they may
well be content with the "Jesus loves me, this I know" level of
story they hear from their Sunday School children. They may
say, feel, and know that "Jesus died for me," and that not
Romans or Jews but *I* put him on the cross—without thinking
through all the implications of atonement and sacrifice.

7. All of which suggests to me that there has to be constant
attention to this subject on all levels, with expectation for an
enjoyment in the small gains that manifestly occur and will
continue to occur. To tell Christians they cannot use the whole
Bible, or that some committee of scholars and interfaith leaders
at a distance blocked out certain passages, would only stir
curiosity and resistance. What is more likely to happen is this:
while the Lectionary does not always have to reproduce as
problematic a text such as the one on which I was expected to
preach, there will be problems in most texts.

Mature, open-minded, adult, struggling, confused Christians will welcome being taken in through the door of the study to the preacher they respect, and to hear her give evidence of her wrestling. They will have regard for "Handle with Care" messages that they hear. They can be educated in empathy, to feel something of what Jews feel when Christian texts that are offensive to them simply get read, celebrated, allowed to work their effect without the critical apprehension of the community. (Community is important: if the text by itself did everything, disband the congregation and have the members disperse to hotel rooms to read and self-interpret the Gideon Bible.)

The sermon that follows is on Mark 7:1–8, 14–15, 21–23 (New Revised Standard Version), an assigned text for the fifteenth Sunday after Pentecost in Series B of a three-year cycle. It is anything but a candidate for "One Hundred Favorite Texts," and presents a real challenge for someone looking for gospel, good news, in the Gospel, the text. I am less clear that I have done justice to the problems it raises for me in respect to the present subject than I am hopeful that it will reveal the ways a preacher wrestles, in order to engage in damage control on the negative side and in the hope that there be a release of liberating energies on the positive. [My word limit having been reached, I ask readers to locate the Gospel of Mark and keep the text before them rather than have me reproduce it.]

A Sermon

During a recent political campaign I was in a metropolis to let the political, not the religious, side of me make a political speech. Like many such speeches, it was held in a black church, specifically an African Methodist Episcopal sanctuary. Protestants, Catholics, Jews, Unitarian Universalists, and secular leaders had signed on as sponsors, their institutions, if any, being listed "for identification purposes only." My co-speaker and I by instinct, training, design, intention, and coaching not only were not to be articulating a Christian theme, but our words were not to be confessionally religious either. Any agnostic, if she held the right political views—namely ours— could have made the speech.

A member of the congregation, a volunteer in the campaign, opened the gathering in the packed church greeting her "fellow Christians." A Muslim reporter covering the event for that city's *The Reader* stomped out, offended by the well-intended but presumptuous inclusion of all there as "fellow Christians." Other volunteers hurried after him: "Wait! Stick around! You don't even know what we'll be doing here . . . "

Two days ago, according to the weekly bulletin, the two Christian congregations that use this space were joined "in our common spiritual ministry in this crucial place" by a Jewish group. If any of these Jews, if any of you, are here on this special nonpolitical occasion and heard me read the Gospel, I would expect you also to be ready to stomp out. It is not easy to be in someone else's shoes, but if I were in theirs, in yours, I'd find it easy to point them to the exit and follow them. In which case this preacher would probably run after you and say: "Wait! Stick around! You don't even know what we'll be doing here . . . "

Of course I would not fault such an escapee-to-be if she kept walking away. This biblical text can easily offend, is offensive, and will remain so unless we provide context and interpretation that will minimize the damage it might do on the way to the positive effects it might work if we explain and apply it.

Then why read it and preach on it? First, because the preacher is a literalist, and it is in the Lectionary, the book of readings assigned for Christian worship in tens of thousands of sanctuaries today. Second, because it is my experience that texts that do not "preach themselves," that do not come easy, usually force us to study, think, probe, and do so much reconceiving that what is potentially positive in them stands a chance of being heard.

Admittedly, using this text is a judgment call, and I could be judged for misjudging it. Admittedly again, including it in the Lectionary was a judgment call by a text or Lectionary committee that does not explain itself. But surely its members must know that with hundreds of pages of Scripture on which to draw, it does not need this one in its 156-Sunday three-year cycle.

To compare judgments, I looked up the passage in a section called "Anti-Jewish Polemic in [the Gospel of Mark]." It appears in a very helpful book on the subject, Norman A. Beck's *Mature Christianity in the 21st Century: The Recognition and Repudiation of the Anti-Jewish Polemic in the New Testament.* Beck posted all the "Keep Off" signs one could need:

This text. . . is the longest controversy dialogue in Mark. . . . This account has all the characteristics of pure polemic of the early church. . . . The response to the question of the Pharisees and scribes can best be described as overkill. . . . What would be required in the translation and in the use of this account in order to direct the criticism of behavior away from the Pharisees and scribes of the first century and to apply it to ourselves within current Christianity where the account will be valid self-critics?

After suggesting a variety of redactions, editing jobs, to redirect the point to the spiritual theme that legitimated its choice, Beck went on:

As a minimum response, 7:1–13 should be removed from our pericope series, which we read in public worship and in preaching, and usage of these verses discouraged in educational and devotional materials. As long as this segment remains as it is in translation texts, anti-Semitism and religious bigotry will continue to be supported by texts that are sacred to Christian people.

He then criticizes the publishers for including the text in the Lectionary and he quotes denominational leadership as intending to be serious: "Christians should make it clear that there is no biblical or theological basis for anti-Semitism. Supposed theological or biblical bases for anti-Semitism are to be examined and repudiated."

Now we have a third reason for my preaching on this: because it is *there*! Because letting it be there and not commenting on it, or letting it be there and expecting each independent reader to be forced to find resources for coping with it seems less creative than airing the theme in public. Still, it takes much interpreting and explaining even here.

Let me preach a few mitigating themes:

— We can assume, we can *know*, that the text was not chosen to promote anti-Judaism today. The record of intent to repent and rectify by the sponsoring denominations and other serious Christian groups is too clear and strong to assume otherwise.

— For those who would make the choice a racial matter, let it be noted that it was written by an unnamed Jew (here named Mark), quoting a Jew, Jesus, quoting a Jew, Isaiah, as part of an evident program to help welcome non-Jews into a still essentially Jewish community.

— If scribes and Pharisees, representing Judaism to ears and eyes then and now, get blasted in Mark, so, and more so, do the disciples of Jesus, presumably representing people now called Christians. It takes forty-five minutes to read the Gospel of Mark. Read it, and if you are a disciple of Jesus, read yourself into it. Not for a split second do any of the disciples ever look good in its sixteen chapters. Peter got called "Satan." Outsiders catch on, but they are foolish, blind, selfish, errant, and out of it. Whoever Mark was and for whatever purpose he wrote, it was not to show the earliest Christian community to be superior to anyone or to give its heirs reason to be prejudiced against anyone.

— Suppose, for a moment, that it was Judaism alone that was being denigrated in this hard-to-read, easy-to-misread chapter. Now bring to the front of your mind what every historian has told you, and can tell you about early Christianity. According to all records, almost at once it was seen to be doing all the things Jesus was criticizing, and failing to be what Jesus, as here heard and speaking, wanted his disciples to be. That is, to quote Isaiah as he did, but now referring to his people, they were quickly and vainly "teaching human precepts as doctrines. "

With those little preliminaries in mind, we may, with caution, tread further into the text and see what controversy and polemic, to which Norman A. Beck referred, was all about. (One of my commentaries has an additional cautionary line that makes it hard for us to crack this text: it "does not greatly impress the modern reader because he or she is not much concerned with the occasion that gave rise to it.") The occasion, according to Mark:

— Jesus' disciples ate with "defiled hands, that is without washing them." The Pharisees and scribes were offended not for this breach of hygiene but of ritual law, an offense against "the tradition of the elders," and thus of something spiritual.

— The scribes and Pharisees did "not eat anything from the market unless they wash it," and Jesus' disciples were accused of eating it "as is." Not health but the equivalent of *kosher*, the set-aside, clean, uncommon as opposed to common issues were at stake.

— "Many other traditions" like the ritual washing of vessels the scribes and Pharisees observed, so they had to ask, "Why do your disciples not live according to the tradition of the elders?"

The Christian commentators try to make things easy by reminding us that the followers of Jesus were offending the oral law, only the comment on law, not the written Law of Moses and thus not the very Law of God. They remind us that Jesus normally kept the Sabbath, but broke it only for humane purpose. I think of a professor who said of another subject, "Take it very, very, very seriously, but not too seriously." Jesus did not come on as an anarchist, as someone simply indifferent, insensitive.

Now it is true, as the commentator said, that it is hard for most of us to read ourselves into the occasion. I don't know a single scribe or Pharisee and rarely run into Jews who want me to wash hands, feet, or pots. But here as so often, comes the exposure of the theme that no doubt led a Lectionary committee to have congregations confront such a text as this, in spite of it all.

Yet there is one more barrier in the verses from Isaiah that Beck thinks could well be dropped from public readings. In it Jesus calls his henceforth passive and silent victims of polemic "you hypocrites," which is not a nice term now and was a horrendous one there and then. In Mark's version, Isaiah thunders judgment on "this people. "

Maybe in a fit of desire to compensate, the Lectionary committee has us read as the first of three readings today Deut. 4:1–2, 6–8, wonderful words about "this people." Israel was to learn the statutes and ordinances of Yahweh and observe them in the land they were to enter and occupy. In awe "the peoples" would then say,

Surely this great nation is a wise and discerning people! For what other great nation has a god so near to it as the Lord our God is whenever we call to him? And what other great nation has statutes and ordinances as just as this entire law that I am setting before you today?

But Mark's Jesus, quoting Isaiah, says of "this people" now what only their own prophets had credentials to say—for Mark speaks across the divide between communities, now as an outsider to Judaism that they "abandon the commandment of God and hold to human tradition. "

What can we mine from all this mixed ore? This is a strange chapter, a dialogue now turned monologue, part of which the Lectionary people mercifully let us skip in public readings. But it leads to a point that in a new context does have a lot to say. Scholars tend to see the subsequent verses as a piecing together of isolated sayings, not in much of a logical sequence. But they do come back to a frequent biblical theme because we get moved from *"things,"* whether these be hands and markets and pots, or texts, to *"persons."* As is so often the case in the Gospels —four early Christian texts—or the gospel—the name Christians use for the whole affirmative action by God through the Jesus who here gets cited the issue is: What kind of a person does Jesus expect and does the gospel produce? And, without much of a stretch, its converse is: What does God, the God witnessed to in encounters like this, expect to see in humans who are responsive to the gospel? Translate again: What is the character of the God who, through Jesus, is revealed in connection with the human character thus described?

The bottom line, according to people who have lived with this text, goes something like this, in paraphrase: the concern here is for cleanliness. In this unfolding, the issue is not whether *things* are or can be unclean or clean; it is *persons* who matter. And they can be defined not by things, but only by themselves, when they act irreligiously and reveal an inward defilement.

This all becomes gospel, good news, when we find a way to experience this cleansed heart. Here comes the uncongenial and admittedly anatomically inexact analogy: in the sayings of Jesus in this Marcan passage we get an important spiritual point through a gross physical metaphor:

Listen to me, all of you, and understand: there is nothing outside a person that by going in can defile, but the things that come out are what defile.

This is, as we said, inexact, of course. Ingested poisons would also defile, in their own distinctive way. But that is not the point of what the disciples call this parable. Now let me cheat a bit to stress the grossness of this all, citing some of the verses the Lectionary committee must have been too squeamish about to have read. Jesus said to the disciples:

> *Then do you also fail to understand? Do you not see that whatever goes into a person from outside cannot defile, since it enters, not the heart but the stomach, and goes out into the sewer?*

That is biblical realism: what comes out—all the "s-words" are signals: sweat, semen, snot, shit, sewerage—is what defiles. There follows a whole catalog of evils that come out to defile; there is no point in repeating them here. The focus is all on a few words: "For it is from within, from the human heart" that unclean or defiling things issue. It is the heart that is at issue. The *changed* heart, the disposition, the inner character matters supremely. The movement is not from without inward, but from within outward. Jesus is saying: if you are an externalist, a thing–person, you will get both things and persons wrong. You are looking out there for the mother of all defilements? Look within.

There is a reach to this advice or proclamation that rings true to Judaism, where the scriptural prayer, also appropriated by Christians, is that God would create a clean heart and renew a right spirit within the person. For the Christian the same prayer is there, now with the distinctive recasting that does not leave the Hebrew Scriptures or the Jews behind, but relates to another version of that heart and spirit. For the disciple of Jesus who reads, who hears this passage, who finds the nugget in all that ore, is not involved only in an intellectual interpretation of old and ambiguous texts. She or he pays attention to the bearer of the message. In Jesus she reads the heart of the one he called "Abba." In the Jesus of self-giving love he sees a mirror of this divine parent. This is the one who issued the divine law, and who allows for "the traditions of the elders" but will not let people be bound by them.

The clean heart is a gift, a treasure. One tends to it, however, as one tends to any kind of treasure: with appreciation, awe, gratitude, and a sense of new responsibility for what is said, for actions, for anything that "comes out of a person," not to defile but to cleanse.

Are you looking out there for the mother of all defilements? Look within.

CHAPTER TWO

Accomplishments and Challenges in the Contemporary Jewish–Christian Encounter

John T. Pawlikowski, O.S.M.

Using Vatican II's *Nostra Aetate* as a benchmark, we are now almost three decades into the contemporary Christian–Jewish encounter. In actual fact the roots of the dialogue go back somewhat earlier as a pioneering generation of biblical scholars, educational researchers, and ecumenists laid the groundwork for that historic document as well as for similar statements in other Christian denominations. But their impact remained rather peripheral until the Council formally launched the process of uprooting the classic theology of Jewish displacement from the covenant in the light of the Christ event and replaced it with a theological work based on the notion of the ongoing validity of the Jewish covenant to which Christians have been joined. We can discern three important phases of the dialogue generated by this document and its attendant Protestant statements. These phases are not entirely sequential in nature; though we stand on the threshold of phase three, not all the crucial work of the first two phases has yet been completed.

Phase one I would describe as the "cleansing" phase. It has primarily affected Christian education. Made possible by the textbook studies on Protestant and Catholic materials at Yale and St. Louis Universities, the impact of these original investigations was significantly aided by the follow-up study of Dr. Eugene Fisher (*Faith Without Prejudice*) which recently has been revised and expanded in a second edition published by the American Interfaith Institute, distributed by Crossroad. This phase has involved the removal from mainline Christian educational texts of the charge that Jews collectively were responsible for the death of Jesus, that the Pharisees were the arch enemies of Jesus and spiritually soulless, that Jews had been displaced by Christians in the covenantal relationship with God as a result of refusal to accept Jesus as the Messiah, that the "Old Testament" was totally inferior to the New and that Jewish faith was rooted in legalism while the Christian religion was based on grace.

This phase is substantially complete as far as it goes for most of the mainline churches. In the case of Catholicism, for example, Dr. Philip Cunningham's recent study at Boston College, confirms the overall improvement in basic educational materials with regard to the principal Jewish stereotypes identified by the St. Louis research team and Dr. Fisher. And the final version of the new catechism has consolidated most of the improvements after serious concerns were raised both by Catholic and Jewish leaders about certain aspects of the preliminary draft. A parallel new study of Protestant materials, still under way, is showing somewhat more mixed results with some of the old stereotypes still in place or even reappearing in certain denominational texts. By and large, we can say that for Catholicism and mainline Protestantism as a whole this "cleansing" phase is nearing completion.

The second phase of the contemporary encounter between Jews and Christians dates back in some ways even further than the textbook studies launched in the late fifties. It is rooted in the new approach to the study of the Hebrew Scriptures and the New Testament which began with several key individuals prior to World War II. Nonetheless this new scholarship really did not achieve a firm foothold until recent years and its overall impact is just beginning to be felt in other dimensions of Church life.

With respect to the study of the Hebrew Scriptures there is ample evidence to suggest that a major shift of emphasis is underway in Christianity. Increasingly respected scholars are recognizing the value of the books of the Hebrew Scriptures in their own right, not merely as a backdrop for New Testament teaching. The commonplace view in the Christian churches for centuries that the "Old Testament" texts are to be considered merely as "foil" or "prelude" for the fundamentally superior teachings found in the Gospels and Epistles is gradually receding.

No one questions the fact that there exists an authentic sense in which these writings serve as important background for understanding the message of Jesus and the New Testament. The question is whether, in addition, we must begin to appreciate in the Hebrew Scriptures revelatory insights which Jesus may have shared as a son of the Torah, but which he did not explicitly proclaim during the years of his public ministry.

It is now becoming increasingly apparent to biblical scholars that the lack of a deep immersion into the spirit and content of the Hebrew Scriptures leaves the contemporary Christian with a truncated version of Jesus' message. In effect, what remains is an emasculated version of biblical spirituality.

Research resulting from the contemporary Christian–Jewish encounter has begun to impact even more profoundly on New Testament interpretation, both with respect to the teachings and person of Jesus and to the pastoral journeys of St. Paul. We are presently witnessing the rapid demise of the virtual stranglehold Rudolf Bultmann and his disciples held over New Testament interpretation for several decades. The Bultmannian school did everything possible to distance Jesus from his concrete ties to biblical and Second Temple Judaism so that he could emerge as a decidedly more "universal" person. Intended or not, such portrayals opened the doors for the development of theological anti-Judaism.

Recent years have seen a profound gravitational shift in New Testament exegesis. Its architects have been scholars such as W. D. Davies, E. P. Sanders, Clemens Thoma, Cardinal Carlo Martini of Milan, James Charlesworth, Daniel Harrington, Robin Scroggs, and others. The list continues to expand. Although they do not agree on every point, these biblical scholars share the conviction that Jesus must be returned to his essentially Jewish context if the Church is to understand his message properly.

Emergence from the Bultmannian perspective is now leading New Testament scholars, according to Professor Robin Scroggs of Union Theological Seminary, to several general conclusions about Jesus and the early Church. Included is the view that the Jesus' movement must be described as a reform movement within Judaism whose members, prior to the war against the Romans, did not have a self-understanding of themselves as a religious community against Judaism.[1]

The significant rethinking of the Jesus' relationship to the Jewish religious tradition has only of late been expanded to include the question of St. Paul's attitude towards Judaism, particularly his attitudes towards Jewish law. Some years ago Bishop Krister Stendahl, a pioneering scholar in this area and then a distinguished member of the Harvard Divinity School faculty, suggested that much of Western Christianity's understanding of the Pauline approach to law had been unduly influenced by its "introspective conscience." This prevailing tendency towards focusing on interior guilt in Western consciousness has colored Christianity's reading of the Pauline literature.

Stendahl's prophetic statement generally went unheeded within the world of biblical scholarship until recent times. Scholars such as E. P. Sanders, James D. G. Dunn, Alan Segal, Lloyd Gaston, and others have now come forward with new studies which challenge the predominant view of Paul's outlook towards Judaism. While most, if not all, of these scholars continue to argue that Paul broke with his fellow Jewish Christians on the issue of Torah observance by Gentiles, the break was not as extreme as customarily understood and his opposition to the law was far more nuanced and circumscribed than was earlier believed. The claimed total opposition to Torah which theologians, especially in the Protestant churches, frequently made the basis for their theological contrast between Christianity and Judaism (freedom/grace vs. Law) now appears to rest on something less than solid ground.

E. P. Sanders' position, while not the identical with the views of all the other scholars working on this question, does introduce distinctions which many now accept as vital for a proper perspective on Paul's evolving outlook towards Torah. Paul had definitely come to the conclusion that ultimately it is God's righteousness through which we are saved. No faithful Jew would in fact challenge this premise. The issue for Paul then came down to two basic questions: (1) do Gentiles need to observe the Torah as a requisite for membership in the covenantal community?; and (2) should Jewish Christians continue to observe Torah? Paul's response to these questions was complex. On one hand, he maintained that in the end only the power of divine righteousness (as now shown in Jesus Christ)

---

1. Chicago Theological Seminary Register, 76.1 (1986), 42–43

can lead the human community to salvation. This was true for both Gentile and Jewish Christians. Hence Paul concluded that observance of the law could not be made a mandatory condition for entry into the Church. But observance of Torah was not necessarily a bad thing in Paul's eyes so long as a person recognizes the primary source of salvation. In fact, some scholars are now persuaded that Paul likely favored the continuation of Torah practice among Jewish Christians. And should a Gentile Christian freely decide to undertake Torah observance there is nothing in Pauline teaching, as now interpreted, to suggest that such a person would be endangering their faith or salvation. Hence, the traditional contrast between Judaism as a religion of law and Christianity as a religion of freedom/grace is profoundly simplistic.

Another significant area of New Testament scholarship that is beginning to show a significant shift in interpretation as a result of Christianity's enhanced understanding of Second Temple Judaism is that of Jesus' parables which are so central in the gospels to his proclamation of the divine reign. Those biblical scholars who in the past down-played Jesus' ties to Judaism also tended to interpret the parables as presenting a message of Jewish displacement from the messianic banquet that was part and parcel of the divine reign. They were also strongly inclined toward maintaining the basic uniqueness of Jesus' parables, ignoring completely parallels in Second Temple Judaism which scholars such as Clemens Thoma, Brad Young, Gordian Marshall, OP, and Michael Hilton have brought to light.

The dominant interpretation of the parables as describing the replacement of the Jews by Christians in the Messianic banquet has played a pivotal role in the shaping of European Catholic theology. The new research on the parables has thus far had modest impact at best on such theologizing, but the potential for substantive transformation remains high.

The mention of systematic theologians in terms of the use of gospel parables leads us directly into the third phase of the Christian–Jewish dialogue, the theological, which still remains a rather fledgling enterprise, peripheral to both mainline Christian and Jewish consciousness. Granted there have been a number of Christian scholars who have undertaken comprehensive studies of the implications of the dialogue, especially

the new biblical research, on Christian theological self-definition. Paul van Buren, A. Roy Eckardt, Peter von der Osten
Sacken, Franz Mussner, and others have made significant contributions in this regard. I have offered my own contributions
in my volumes *Christ in the Light of the Christian Jewish Dialogue*
and *Jesus and the Theology of Israel*. On the Jewish side a few
scholars such as Irving Greenberg, David Novak, Michael
Wyschogrod, Leon Klenicki, and Norman Solomon have
examined the question in terms of Jewish self-understanding.
But on the whole these have failed to penetrate the theological
mainstream in the churches.

Major figures such as David Tracy and Johannes Metz have
recognized the importance of the Christian–Jewish dialogue
and the new understanding of Jesus' relationship with Judaism
for all of Christian theology, not just for conversations with
Jews, for they are very much in the minority. And even their
work is not totally consistent in applying this principle. Some
promise appears, however, in the recent work of Jurgen
Moltmann who has attempted, whether successfully or not is a
matter of some controversy, to apply the new insights from the
Christian–Jewish dialogue to the core of his theological presentation. This stands in marked contrast to the voluminous
work of Hans Küng on Judaism which, while it has many com-
mendable features (particularly in its treatment of anti-
Semitism), fails almost completely in terms of applying the
new biblical picture of Jesus and Judaism to his basic articula-
tion of Christian faith, especially Christology.

And when one examines official ecclesial documents whether
denominational or ecumenical the picture that emerges thus far
is rather bleak. The Catholic conciliar statement and its follow-
up documents in 1974 and 1985 and the several forward looking statements by Pope John Paul II rarely, if ever, find their way
into other documents when the church is attempting to state its
own self-definition. The picture within the World Council of
Churches is not much different. This situation tends to convey
the impression, falsely or not, that these are statements the
churches make only when speaking with Jews and not when
engaged in self reflection and internal education. We cannot say
Christian–Jewish dialogue has arrived until such time as the
statements from the dialogue become internally commonplace
in Christianity whether any Jew is present or not.

A ray of hope did appear in this context in 1993. In preparation for the International Meeting on Ecumenism which periodically brings together Catholic, Protestant, and Orthodox Christians, a draft statement was prepared in Dublin. This Dublin document was typical in its neglect of the Jewish question and its failure to utilize any of the documents from the Christian–Jewish dialogue despite the language of many of these statements about an intimate bonding between Jews and Christians at the very heart of the church's self-identity. In at least one section the text came very close to advocating the discredited "displacement theology" of Judaism. After interventions were made from North America and Europe important changes were made in the Stuttgart revision (for presentation to the meeting at Santiago de Compostela, Spain) which eliminated the most troublesome section and made a minimal effort to develop the note of bondedness.

Finally, a word about the area of liturgy and worship where theological statement is communicated to the Christian faithful. Thus far we have only scratched the surface in this area. Removing terms such as "perfidious Jews" from the Good Friday service in Catholicism, while important symbolically, strikes only at the tip of the problem. The fundamental structure of so many of our major liturgical seasons revolves around the simplistic "prophecy/fulfillment" theme that theologians are discarding. This presents a major challenge that requires the wholesale attention of liturgists. The operative principle for liturgy must become, "Do liturgical celebrations promote within the worshipping community a sense of the continued, deep bonding between Jews and Christians that has been a paramount feature of most recent Christian theological statements emanating from the dialogue with Jews?" Anything short of this ultimately fails the standards which *Nostra Aetate* and other documents have introduced.

In summary, we can say that major changes have been made and continue to develop in the church's understanding of Jews and Judaism. The biggest advances have occurred in textbooks and in scriptural exegesis. The areas of systematic theology, ethics, and liturgy still await necessary major surgery.

CHAPTER THREE

Interpreting Difficult Texts

Clark M. Willlamson and Ronald J. Allen

Anti-Judaism is a systematic hermeneutical strategy which Christians have too often and too long used in interpreting for each other the meaning of the Christian faith. Anti-Judaism is not merely a theme that may or may not appear in the writings of church leaders. It is a way of understanding all the other themes in the arsenal of Christian reflection: God, Christ, covenant, Scripture, the Holy Spirit, to name but a few. Of particular concern to preachers is the fact that anti-Judaism as a way of interpreting Scripture can be incredibly effective in preaching. What needs to be noticed about anti-Judaism is that it never was merely "armchair" theology. It appears in the history of the church in tracts that are intended to form Christian identity, to provide counsel for how Christians are to behave toward their Jewish neighbors, to organize and define the boundaries of the Christian community, and to give pastoral guidance. The function of anti-Judaism in shaping Christian social identity, behavior, attitudes, and feelings has been considerably effective.

Throughout Christian history and continuing into the present, the sermon has been *the* most efficacious way to generate and keep alive anti-Jewish attitudes and feelings in Christian congregations. In our book, *Interpreting Difficult Texts* (Philadelphia: Trinity Press International, 1989), we include a chapter surveying the history of Christian preaching to back up this point as incontrovertibly as possible.

The great difficulty in addressing the role of anti-Judaism in Christian preaching today is that by and large anti-Judaism survives in preaching in ways of which preachers are, it can be assumed, largely unaware. By contrast, when we read the eight sermons preached by Chrysostom in late fourth-century Antioch or Luther's dying plea that all Jews be expelled from Saxony, we know that Chrysostom and Luther intended to say what they said. Theirs was an intentional, conscious anti-Judaism.

In the so-called mainline churches of today, however, what seems to be the case is that anti-Judaism survives as an ideology in the more proper sense of the term, i.e., one of which its practitioners are not conscious. In workshops that we have run on anti-Judaism and preaching, we describe what anti-Judaism in Christian preaching sounds like and often elicit from well intentioned pastors the embarrassed confession: "I can remember having preached that sermon myself." In the section of our chapter devoted to preaching in twentieth-century America, we discovered a general decline in anti-Judaism early in the century in the preaching of Protestant liberals and modernists. Unfortunately, this decline went hand-in-hand with a decline in attention to biblical texts and with a rise in preaching topical sermons for which the text was usually little more than a jumping-off point from which the sermon could be launched.

However, with the impact of the biblical theology movement on preachers and more attention to biblical texts, we noted a corresponding increase of anti-Judaism in sermons. So, at least, it appeared to us from our reading of sermons selected as high in quality and published in pulpit journals. What seems to have been going on is that the polemic that surfaces in New Testament texts was often uncritically repeated in the sermon as the pastor "preached the text."

One change in our thinking since we wrote *Interpreting Difficult Texts* is that we would not speak as freely now as we did then of "anti-Judaism" in the New Testament. It is, of course, anachronistic to attribute modern, racist anti-Semitism to the New Testament. Nor should we retroject onto the New Testament attitudes from the third and fourth centuries. A set of terms something like that devised by George M. Smiga, who distinguishes among "prophetic polemic," "subordinating polemic," and "abrogating anti-Judaism" and finds each in some places in the New Testament is helpful to this discussion.[1] The value of historical–critical approaches that analyze polemic in the New Testament is that they enable us to see this polemic as relative to the first-century context in which it was congenital and so to set it aside.[2]

Two points about preaching must be noted. One is the effect that preaching has upon its hearers. With regard to anti-Judaism, the social dynamic at work in those exposed to anti-Jewish preaching seems to be that the more negative images parishioners receive about Jews of long ago, the more they tend (statistically, not necessarily) to project these images onto their Jewish neighbors.[3] In this connection, the way the Christian faith is preached and taught in church is seen as second only to a lack of education as a source of contemporary anti-Semitism.[4] Second, with respect to the task of preaching, the crucial issue is two fold: how preachers shall make responsible use of better historical understandings of the entire context surrounding Jesus and Paul, and consequently of what Jesus and Paul were about, and how they shall interpret for their congregations the hostility and polemics that surface in certain texts.

There is a burgeoning amount of recent New Testament scholarship that does a better job of seeing Jesus and Paul in context than we have ever had in the history of the church.[5] Seminary students should be exposed to this literature in introductory courses in New Testament and homiletics students should not be allowed to forget it. What we say about Jesus and Paul should, at minimum, be appropriate to those about whom we speak.

Historical–critical thinking, however, is essential to the

1. See George M. Smiga, *Pain and Polemic* (New York: Paulist Press, 1992), pp. 18–23.
2. Luke T. Johnson's "The New Testament's Anti-Jewish Slander and the Conventions of Ancient Polemic," *JBL* 108 (1989), 419–441, is an excellent example of this kind of study.
3. For a study of the attitudes of clergy and how lay people learn prejudice from clergy, see Rodney Stark, Bruce D. Foster, Charles Y. Glock, and Harold E. Quinley, *Wayward Shepherds: Prejudice and the Protestant Clergy* (New York: Harper & Row, 1971). Of course, not all clergy are culpable in this regard.
4. See particularly the analysis in Harold E. Quinley and Charles Y. Glock, *Anti-Semitism in America* (New York: The Free Press, 1979), pp. 22–27.
5. We refer the reader to only a few of these excellent works: James H. Charlesworth, *Jesus Within Judaism* (New York: Doubleday, 1988), Paula Fredriksen, *From Jesus to Christ* (New Haven: Yale University Press, 1988), and E. P. Sanders, *Jesus and Judaism* (Philadelphia: Fortress Press, 1985).

preparation for preaching. Preaching itself should interpret for congregants the meaning of the Christian faith; it is at heart a hermeneutical enterprise. And here is where the rub comes. The inherited anti-Jewish reading of Jesus, which is usually simply part of the furniture of the church in which those who become preachers are socialized, sees his teaching as against Jews and Judaism, his life as lived out in conflict with Jews and Judaism, and his death as having taken place at the hands of Jews and Judaism. The clash between Jesus and Judaism is often taken as so sharp that his crucifixion is interpreted as the necessary result of it: he was crucified by Jews and Judaism. Yet, God raised him from the dead in victory over Jews and Judaism.

There are at least four themes that appear prominently in anti-Jewish preaching. The most pervasive and simplest is the one that trades on negative images of Jews and Judaism in the Gospels, the Book of Acts and, in some ways, Hebrews. According to this theme, Jews and Judaism serve as the images of everything bad in religion. The tendency among the redactors of the gospels increasingly to set the sayings of Jesus within the context of controversy with Jews can easily be picked up in sermons and exaggerated. The fact that Mark's real enemies were probably not Jews but the authority figures of the more conservative Jerusalem church, with Pharisees, e.g., appearing as "fictive" opponents is missed or glossed over and harmful stereotypes of Jews repeated.

More particular ways of specifying these negative images are to accuse Jews and Judaism of being adamantly committed to what is old, past, and gone, of being more concerned with the letter of the law than with the more genuinely inward or spiritual dimension of religion, or of being hooked on law, works, rewards, and merit rather than grace and love. This polemic tends to catch Jews in a no-win situation: if they keep the law, they are works righteous; if they do not they are hypocritical. Concern with name calling sometimes spoils an otherwise good teaching, as when the commandment to "judge not, that you be not judged" (Matt. 7:1) is shortly followed with the address: "You hypocrite!" (Matt. 7:5). The sermon based on this passage can result in a mixed message of the sort that says: "Quit name calling, Jerk!"

This theme is of a piece with the next, which heaps mounds

of criticism upon Jews and Judaism and leaves Christians with the impression, whether tacit or overt, that with us everything is quite alright. Not only does this theme compound the harm of the first of perpetuating pejorative images of Jews and Judaism, it deprives the church of the capacity for prophetic self-criticism, a capability that is a great strength of the Jewish tradition.

Third is the displacement/replacement theme, that might also be called the "salvation through Jesus Christ alone" motif. The tendency of preachers to expropriate the name "Israel" for the church and to regard the church as the "new Israel" (in spite of the absence of this term from the New Testament) that replaces "old Israel" abets this motif. Sometimes the universalism or inclusivism, a term much in vogue these days, is contrasted with the unfortunate particularism or exclusivism of the Jews. It is difficult to differentiate this kind of inclusivism from sectarianism directed against Jews.

The last theme results as much as anything else from the overall impression that an uncritical reading of the Gospels may make on preachers. The conflict theme, while not the only way of portraying the relationship between Jesus and various other kinds of Jews in the Gospels, easily becomes predominant in their exposition and interpretation. At this point, literary criticism can at least alert us to a profound and subtle difficulty. Jack Dean Kingsbury, for example, sees the theme of conflict as not only "central to the plot of Matthew," but argues that the leaders of Israel are presented there as "implacable adversaries" of Jesus. The conflict is so acrid that only Jesus and his apostles come across as "real people." Jewish leaders and crowds are depicted as "flat characters."[6]

If preaching similarly depicts Jewish figures as at best stick figures lacking any depth, complexity of feeling and thought, or beauty of heart and soul, where might churchpeople learn that, indeed, Jews are real human beings?

To counteract and overcome the impact of anti-Judaism on preaching, we propose an interrelated set of hermeneutical and homiletical moves. Hermeneutically, we suggest that pastors avail themselves of the attempt of the Protestant Reformers to

---

6. Jack Dean Kingsbury, *Matthew as Story* (Philadelphia: Fortress Press, 1986), pp. 3–10.

come up with a norm for interpreting Scripture, a norm that stands in the service of freedom. Assuredly, we also suggest that preachers employ this norm consistently which, had they done it, would have prevented the Reformers from falling into anti-Jewish rhetoric. The freedom spoken of here is twofold. One is the freedom of the interpreter to understand Scripture responsibly even when a given text may be laden with polemic. The other is the freedom of God to be gracious to whomever God chooses to be gracious. The first point holds that exposition of a text does not assure the preaching of a message that will build up persons in authentic faith, be appropriate to the good news, or be morally credible with regard to the attitudes it suggests about our neighbors. The second contends that Jesus Christ is a gift to the church from the unconditional love of the God of Israel. However, we may not take that gift and turn it into a condition by which God is not free to love those who are different from us, specifically Jews. It also holds that if Jesus Christ is the gift to the church from the God of Israel, he is also a gift from the Israel of God in whom he took shape.

Furthermore, we make two hermeneutical suggestions: that the good news or word of God manifest in the New Testament is a re-presentation of the *same* word made known by God to Israel in history, in the Torah, and in the prophets. The word of God in Jesus Christ is not some historical novelty to which Jews should convert; it is new in precisely the sense of being the primordial word of God to Israel and therefore always new and always renewing. And we borrow the suggestion from James Sanders' "canonical criticism" that preachers interpret Scripture by exactly the same hermeneutical axioms in terms of which Scripture interprets itself.[7] These axioms stress that God is one (the monotheizing axiom), that God loves you or this particular community, perhaps exclusively (the constitutive axiom) and that God loves all others in precisely the same way (the prophetic axiom). It is important to note that if we operate with only the constitutive axiom the result is idolatry: God loves me/us and no one else, and that if we operate exclusively with the prophetic axiom the result is self-emptying: God

---

7. For the original source here see James Sanders, *Canon and Community: A Guide to Canonical Criticism* (Philadelphia: Fortress Press, 1984).

loves all the others but not me/us. The gospel is the promise/gift of God's love to each and all, the fact that we are so loved commands that we in turn love God with all our selves and our neighbors as ourselves. One can see such an interpretive move being made in Scripture itself by such a passage as this: "For we hold that a person is justified by faith apart from works prescribed by the law. Or is God the God of Jews only? Is he not the God of Gentiles also? Yes of Gentiles also, since God is one; and he will justify the circumcised on the ground of faith and the uncircumcised through that same faith" (Rom. 3:28–30). These hermeneutical approaches require us to criticize ideology in ourselves and in Scripture, i.e., to see where ideas promote the interests of a group, defend the group against others, or call for the use of power over other groups.

Homiletically we argue that New Testament texts fall loosely into three groups insofar as their attitudes and tone toward Jews and Judaism are concerned. Some texts proclaim good news for both Jews and Christians. Others, in spite of their original meaning, have been interpreted so consistently in anti-Jewish ways that they need to undergo reinterpretation if the good news in them is to be made clear to the congregation. A third group simply presents good news for Christians at the expense of bad news for Jews. These texts need to be dealt with directly in preaching and teaching, and corrected. Sometimes, we suggest, preachers must have the courage to preach "against the text." Not everything in the Bible is biblical. Some of the texts most in need of correction tend to appear in the lectionary late in Lent and around Passion Sunday, Good Friday, and Holy Week.

Throughout all this, we assume some things. We assume that the purpose of the church is to spread in the world the love of God and the love of the neighbor. We assume that love of the neighbor is meaningless unless we see to it, minimally, that our preaching does no harm to the neighbor and, more fully, that it actively promotes good will. We assume that what happens in church on Sunday morning is important and therefore that it is important to see to it that what happens there is genuinely appropriate to the Christian faith and that it is morally credible. We assume that the purpose of preaching is to build up the whole people of God, not to tear down Jews with whom Christians are no more than fellow citizens among one people.

CHAPTER FOUR

Christian Preaching after the Holocaust

Harry James Cargas

Since the end of World War II have had the opportunity to hear well over two thousand homilies in Catholic churches throughout America. Never have I heard one on Jewish–Christian relations. I have listened to men in the pulpit try to explain why it is a sin for men to wear bermuda shorts, why nuns who choose to abandon traditional religious garb were actually playing into the hands of the Communists, even one that began "Whenever we think of Easter, we think of the Easter bunny." This last example is galling in a particular way. Easter is a Christian feast celebrated to commemorate Jesus' victory over death, through his resurrection, and thus the possible salvation of all of us. It is the one day of the year that all Catholics, the fully loyal, and those who have not practiced their religious "obligations" faithfully, are expected to attend Mass. Redemption from death and hell is presumably serious stuff. The priest knows that many in the pews that day are irregulars; here is perhaps his one chance to impart a spiritual message to his flock for a whole year. And what was the lesson of the day on the Sunday I'm speaking of? "You're no bunny 'til some bunny loves you." The priest proved to be a good fellow, one of us, going for laughs. He wasn't about to burden us with any troubling theological insights. Easter is for eggs and chocolates and bonnets and oh yes, triumph over death.

Our era is the time after the Holocaust. Why has that awesome event registered so little with our ordained Christian preachers? Why can't we, whose religious obligation includes repenting our sins, acknowledge that probably every killer of Jews in the Shoah—every single murderer—was a baptized Christian? And it takes a lot of people to kill a lot of people. Thousands of people at least, who called themselves Christians, massacred countless numbers of Jews, Romani (as Gypsies prefer to be called), Jehovah's Witnesses, homosexuals, and others. Hundreds of millions stood by in the world and allowed it to happen. How could this have been so? Why is my Church silent and therefore its churches silent over the greatest sin in our history?

None of this is to imply collective guilt, of course. Those not yet born during the war, those who did not persecute or stand "neutrally" by, or were themselves victims, or who did resist the policies of Nazis and others are clearly not culpable. But we Christians who do not renounce what the Holocaust was all about, who are willfully ignorant of the background, the event, and its implications are in danger of being post-Holocaust accomplices. We are in danger of continuing the iniquitous convention of anti-Semitism and thus, at it's very roots, anti-Christianity. One cannot hate and be a Christian at the same time. Unfortunately, some hate and *call* themselves Christian, but that is an impossible pairing.

What then is necessary to be done? (Because it is so rooted in the soil of Christian custom). The ignorance of anti-Judaism will persevere until it is drowned out by the water of religious enlightenment. The scapegoating idea that Jews were responsible for the death of Jesus is both bad history and bad theology. Nevertheless for centuries Christians were able to blame Jews (collectively no less) for the crucifixion without much fear of contradiction. Today it is somewhat different, especially for Catholics. *Somewhat* different. We have in our more contemporary religious repertoire, as it were, Vatican II and *Nostrae Aetate*, both of which specifically condemned anti-Semitism. But while theologians and some others are fully cognizant of what this means for Christians it might not be too much to say that most Catholics and other Christians are only vaguely aware of the implications, some are fully unaware, and some even prefer to ignore these teachings. Yet, perhaps unlike certain Vatican documents, there is no ambiguity of statement here. Two sentences from *Nostra Aetate* (issued October 28, 1965) will suffice: Moreover, mindful of her common patrimony with the Jews, and motivated by the gospel's spiritual love and by no political considerations, she deplores the hatred, persecution, and displays of anti-Semitism directed against the Jews at any time and from any source.

"So we return to the questions: "What then is necessary to be done? "

The very first step that Christians must take to become reconciled with Jews after the Holocaust is the acknowledged role that Christianity in general and Christians in particular had in the monstrous tragedy. And along with admitting what truly happened (or did not happen in the case of those who stood by and did nothing) must go repentance. A large part of Christian spiritual activity must be in the form of repentance. In both the Testament adapted from the Jews and the Christian Testament, the concept of repentance for sins is prominent. Repentance signifies a change of mind or heart and connotes regret for one's past transgressions. Usually this is accompanied by acts of penance meant to atone for the sins committed. Such acknowledgment should be preached to the faithful. Our model for repentance is none other then God who "repented of the evil which he thought to do unto his people" (Ex 32:14); and again in Jer 18:8, where God speaks of repenting. The Israelites are urged to repent in 1 Kgs 8:47 as they are in Ez 14:6 where we read "Repent . . . and turn away your faces from all abominations."

The specifically Christian text has its equal insistence: ". . . except you repent, you shall all likewise perish" (Lk 13:3); and at least another dozen references to repentance including "Remember therefore from what you have fallen, and repent . . ." (Rv 2:5). This must become ever apparent in Christian thinking about the Holocaust and nowhere more than in the Sunday instructions given in the worship services. Thus it is imperative that Christian seminaries require that their students study the history and implications of anti-Judaism in general and of the Holocaust in particular. Many ministers and priests are shockingly ignorant of both the facts surrounding the negative attitudes towards Jews held by Christians for centuries as well as the dreadful specifics of the World War II massacre of so many millions of people who had their religious roots in the soil of Christendom. This situation needs radical modification if anti-Judaism is to be eliminated. But if the ministers know little about the history and theology of religious anti-Semitism, they cannot work to eradicate it. Future clergy have got to know how important this subject is. If it is not insisted upon in the seminaries, how can they be expected to comprehend its gravity?

To insure a sharing of the vision of Jewish–Christian brotherhood and sisterhood the liturgical calendars of the various Christian denominations should include an annual service dedicated to remembering the Holocaust. This will both inspire members of the Christian community to think and pray about the victims and the criminals, the policies and unconcern of so many, and it will also be a sign to Jews that Christians are beginning to care enough to take the Shoah seriously on the congregational level as well as the more scholarly theological level. Christianity is, among other things, a religion of symbols. If we would begin to make moves in the direction of reconciliation—especially in the area of public preaching—it would signify to Jews that we are serious about the issue of Jewish Christian relations. Furthermore, it would give a message to neo-Nazis, the Klan, certain skinheads (not all are racist or violent, some are merely registering social protest in a particular way) and anti-Semites of various ilk that their behavior is morally intolerable.

There are important topics that will have to be addressed during these liturgical teachings, as well as at other times. One is a reminder to congregations of the essential Jewishness of Christianity. As I have written elsewhere, "This point will need elaboration only for the theologically retarded." We can add to this the danger that anti-Semitism holds for the Christian's soul. We can recall the teachings of Dr. Martin Luther King, Jr., who warned us of how hatred warps the soul of the hater, how in the long run, racism is more destructive to the racist than to the racist's targets. It might be instructive for preachers to consider what has happened to the Christian psyche over the centuries. Christians glory in an inheritance of love, sacrifice, good works, and even martyrdom. And yet under some Christians, Jews, and others too have endured persecution, exile, ghettoization, imprisonment, torture, and murder. Are we currently passing on any part of our legacy— glorious or evil—to our children, our community, our unborn generations?

What follows is logical: any recognition of the Jewish roots of Christianity should pave the way for a discussion of Jesus as a link (rather than a divisive figure) between Christians and Jews. Perhaps it was stated most authoritatively in this country in a document written under the dual sponsorship of the Commission on Faith and Order of the National Council of Churches and the Secretariat for Catholic–Jewish Relations of the National Conference of Catholic Bishops of which here is an excerpt:

> The Church of Christ is rooted in the life of the People of Israel.
> We Christians look upon Abraham as our spiritual ancestor and father of our faith. . . .
> The ministry of Jesus and the life of the early Christian community were thoroughly rooted in the Judaism of their day, particularly in the teachings of the Pharisees.
> The Christian faith is still sustained by the living faith of the patriarchs and the prophets, kings and priests, scribes and rabbis, and the people whom God chose for his own. Christ is the link . . . enabling the Gentiles to be numbered among Abraham's "offspring" and therefore fellow heirs with the Jews according to God's promise.
> It is a tragedy of history that Jesus, our bond of unity with the Jews, has all too often become a symbol and source of division and bitterness because of human weakness and pride.

These words, so important for our discussion, for our faith, are basically unknown to many people, thus underscoring the need for seminar courses in the theological relationship of Judaism and Christianity so that such information can be shared.

For preachers to go deeper, it will be necessary for them to examine the idea of inspiration in Christian Scripture. This is threatening territory to many (and, again, seminary attention to a subject like this might prove ideal). Christians should not fear such a question, however. The person on whom their faith has been founded urged a search for truth, insisting that "The truth shall make you free." Gregory Baum wrote this as a priest: "If the Church wants to clear itself of the anti-Jewish trends built into its teaching, a few marginal correctives will not do. It must examine the very center of its proclamation and reinterpret the meaning of the gospel for our times." He recognizes the impact of the Holocaust on this thought when he adds that "what the encounter of Auschwitz demands of Christian theologians, therefore, is that they submit Christian teaching to a radical ideological critique." Among the questions to be considered are these: Are we misinterpreting the passages in the Christian Bible which appear to be anti-Semitic? Have certain words in Scripture been added to the original texts as some scholars would have it? Are the anti-Semitic passages really there and if so how are we to regard them today?

As apart of the close investigation of Scripture called for, pastors and others need to find new terminology for what many now call the Old Testament and the New Testament. These are actually titles which are insulting to Jews. The titles imply a kind of arrogance: Christians have appropriated (most of) the Jewish texts and adopted them to their own interpretation. They have updated the Jewish Book and have given their own explication to the meaning of events. The terms can be better signified—perhaps the designation "Apostolic Writings" as suggested by Father John Pawlikowski would serve for the Christian texts and "Hebrew Scriptures" would make it clear that the earlier writings belong to a separate religious tradition, but are shared by Christians. That might prove a beginning.

Most of the Christian pulpits are not available to women at this time and that is another area where improvements in the area of Jewish–Christian relations could easily be effected. Without women ministers, churches prohibit to themselves a feminine perspective on every theological topic imaginable. Would not women's points of view on the hatred preached or ignored by male preachers have given the Christian world a more Christian attitude toward those now seen to be brothers and sisters in faith? Why is there a restriction keeping women from the pulpit? Let the sermon time be open to the laity, women and men, especially those competent to speak on the history and meaning of Christian relations (including antagonism) with the Jewish people.

Finally, attempts by Christians to convert Jews to their faith must not only be abandoned but also discouraged by the preachers in the churches. Behind every missionary attempt is the usually unstated belief that we have the total truth; you have almost none. This, again, is a position of arrogance. The energy I use to convert a Jew would be better spent in perfecting my own spiritual life. Let one major example illustrate the direction that needs to be taken here. In 1846, a new religious order was founded by two brothers who themselves converted to Catholicism from Judaism.

Marie Alphonse and Marie Theodore Ratisbonne established the Congregation of Notre Dame de Sion for the purpose of bringing about a better understanding between Jews and Christians and for the conversion of the former. Today, however, the goal of that order has changed. The followers of the Ratisbonnes insist that proselytizing must be completely abandoned, and they have become leaders in trying to bring members of both religious groups together in mutual understanding based on equality and total respect.

These are some suggestions for steps Christians can take to begin to become reconciled with Jews. It will take a long time; centuries of persecution will not be healed in a decade. But we must begin, collectively and individually. What will Jews do in response? That is a question that Christians need not ask. No matter how Jews receive our belated overtures, our own conversions to a Christianity free of anti-Semitism, we Christians must make the effort to be virtuous, to be open, to be loving. If we do, only good things can follow.

CHAPTER FIVE

Removing Anti-Judaism From the Pulpit: Four Approaches

Robert J. Daly, S.J.

"Removing anti-Judaism from the pulpit" is, in this post-Holocaust era, one of the most profoundly urgent of Christian tasks. From the Roman Catholic perspective from which I write, it is a task that is both simple and complex. On the various levels of doctrine and of liturgical, disciplinary, and pastoral directives, the task is relatively simple. Since the time of Vatican II, a series of declarations, statements, and directives, as well as various actions taken by several popes, have exposed the old anti-Jewish myths for the murderous lies that they are, and highlighted the sacred bonds of kinship and the common gifts of grace and election shared by members of the Christian and Jewish communities. In addition, the more scholarship has opened up to modern eyes the shape and the feel of the ancient worlds from which Judaism and Christianity came, and the more historians have viewed the past from several and not just from one biased point of view, the more has it become clear that Judaism and Christianity are, whenever they are true to themselves, inextricably bound up in each other's fate and destiny. Expressed bluntly from the Christian perspective, to be anti-Jewish is to be anti-Christian.[1]

Both in the official teaching of the Roman Catholic Church and in the scholarly research which Catholics share with others in the academic community, this has been expressed so

---

1. For references and suggestions for further reading, see the bibliographic note at the end of this article

clearly and unambiguously that the theoretical task of "removing anti-Judaism from the pulpit" is relatively simple. The case doesn't have to be made that this is what Catholic preachers of the Word of God must do. The complexity is encountered when one tries to achieve this end in actual homiletic practice. The major cause of the difficulty seems to lie in a widespread popular perception that the New Testament, the Gospels, and especially the Gospel of John, are themselves somewhat anti-Jewish. Thus the problem is serious, and it lies at the heart of Christian self-identity. For if most Christians (I wish I were able to say: "if *some* Christians") read and hear the Gospels as anti-Jewish, our task is indeed massive. More so perhaps in those churches which do not have the kind of strong church teaching authority on which, in instances such as this, Catholics can rely. But in the end, the task is the same: How is the preacher to deal with scriptural passages which, when read from the pulpit, strike most hearers as anti-Jewish?

From what I have said about recent teaching of the Catholic Church on this matter, one might expect to find the beginning of an answer in the way recent products of Catholic seminaries are preaching the Word. In contrast to older priests, their religious and theological formation has taken place in a time when the essential anti-Christianity of anti-Judaism had already become part of the official Catholic position. But alas, one finds that they too are still part of the problem. They do not, of course, preach an anti-Judaism as some in the past might have done; they might even effectively preach against it on those all too rare occasions when it is the topic they are developing. But characteristically, the seemingly anti-Jewish implications of many New Testament texts remain uncommented upon, unchallenged. Homiletic preparation, apparently, even in the best of seminaries, has not caught up to the Church's official teaching.

It is easy to identify the Lectionary as one of the causes of the problem, for it is indeed filled with passages of seemingly anti-Jewish tenor. But no easy solution is found by looking there. Reorganizing the Lectionary might admittedly bring some improvement; but if one were to eliminate all possibly offensive passages, one would indeed be flushing away the baby with the bath. The challenge of apparent anti-Jewishness in Scripture must be met head on. We have to find ways to deal with the situation in homiletically constructive ways and at the same time to do this without making such a big deal of it that everything is reduced to just this theme. In this essay I will presume general agreement on what we should be doing and focus my attention on four practical ways how to do it.

1. The first is the obvious, direct method: a sermon devoted specifically to the theme of anti-Judaism. In the first instance, but not necessarily as the first order of business, depending on the specific pastoral and homiletic situation, one should draw upon the "teaching" and the resources that are available in one's own church tradition. For Roman Catholics, that is relatively simple, as I have indicated. But even the more evangelically oriented, the more "free church" traditions, have resources within them which can be brought to bear on this issue. I would suggest that these be milked as much as possible, precisely as an antidote to the (often implicit, unconscious) anti-Jewish bias that thrives unchallenged within so many church traditions.

Becoming more specific, especially in light of the fact that this particular point has still not been picked up by so many Christians, one cannot emphasize too strongly that supersessionism—the doctrine that God's covenant with Israel has been abrogated and rendered worthless by the new covenant in Jesus Christ—is no longer, at least not in the Roman Catholic and similar traditions, an acceptable Christian position. However, the individual Christian preacher, even in those traditions which have turned away from supersessionism, must give careful thought to how this should be preached. They might even have to decide that it should not be preached head on. For it is an obvious fact that many Christians still think that supersessionism is divinely revealed. Any challenge to supersessionism would strike them as equivalent to denying the validity of Christianity itself. If care is not exercised, speaking against supersessionism could as easily alienate as win over such hearers of the Word.

Perhaps a bit easier point to make will be that the Jews are not the murderers of Jesus, however much some Christians of the past may have thought so. To claim that Jews are "Christkillers" or "God-murderers" is itself a murderous lie, at least in the sense that it seems to have had murderous effects on the minds, for example, of those medieval crusaders who thought that they were doing something "Christian" as they wiped out some Rhineland Jewish communities while on their way to the Holy Land. The same murderous effect has apparently been operative in our own century as well, for example, in the apathy of so many Christians (and not just German Christians) in the face of the Holocaust. To drive home this point, the homilist can draw upon three sources: church teaching, where available, historical–critical research, and a careful, direct reading of the New Testament itself.

Another resource for the thematic sermon against anti-Judaism is historical context. Historical context demonstrates how thoroughly Jewish—one might even say how essentially Jewish—were Jesus and the first Christians. Historical context locates the final literary composition of the New Testament Gospels at a time when the Jewish and the Jewish–Christian communities were beginning to perceive each other as enemies and points out that that perception influences the wording of the Gospels. Historical context points out the presence in the New Testament of a style of vigorously (to our minds even violently) antagonistic apologetics, even between parties—e.g., Jesus and the scribes and Pharisees—which actually accepted each other as fraternal coreligionists. Take away historical context and the hearer of the biblical Word inevitably hears Jesus and the Jews, Jesus and the scribes and Pharisees, vigorously attacking each other. That seemingly violent antagonism is, in an nonhistorical context, inevitably projected onto the Jews and the Judaisms of all times and places. Add historical context and all of the perceived violence and much of the sharpness disappears.

Historical context, however, is not an easy tool for the homilist to use. In the first instance it does require something of the skill of a scholar. Most preachers have some, but unfortunately—or is it fortunately?—not a great deal of scholarship. And in any case, scholarly disquisitions are not the stuff of which good sermons are made. In the second instance, historical contextualizing is perceived by many Christians as a reduction of the biblical word to something less than a divinely inspired word. Preachers who unwarily take up the tool of historical criticism will find that they have stepped into a dangerous minefield. Nevertheless, and precisely on this point, the preacher must be guided by good scholarship; for scholarship, while alone insufficient for good preaching, is one of the indispensable antidotes to the poisonous anti-Judaism that is one of Christianity's greatest scandals.

Taking up the more positive side, a thematic sermon on this topic needs to emphasize and illustrate as strongly and as clearly as possible the Jewishness of Jesus. Jesus, Joseph, and Mary, all the Apostles and first disciples, were all Jews. And to make the point more bluntly, they were Jews of the pharisaic kind. The idea that the Christianity of Jesus' followers and the Judaism of the Pharisees were essentially antagonistic is a myth that has been demolished by modern historical research. The first followers of Jesus were Jews of the pharisaic kind. If one wants to understand Jesus and Paul, one must first understand the kind of Jewish devotional life that was inculcated by the Pharisees and which nourished the human religious development of Jesus himself.

From the more strictly theological side, the sermon addressing this theme can draw powerful arguments from the central Christian mystery of the Incarnation. In the full, space–time sense of the word, God became human once, and only once. That was in Jesus, a Palestinian Jew, the son of Joseph and Mary of Nazareth. This is, from the Christian perspective, the transcendently sacred, central point of human history. This is the one most certain point at which God became a flesh and blood, space and time part of our human existence; and God did this "for us and for our salvation" in the Jew, Jesus of Nazareth. It is from Jesus the Jew and from his Jewishness that there comes to us all that is most sacred, most loving, most healing, and most forgiving, all that is most directly promising of the eternal life of God for which we yearn.

In other words, that wry British verse that goes: "How odd of God to choose the Jews" has got it completely backwards. Looked at now, after the fact, aware of how gloriously we are blessed through Jesus the Jew, we must rather, with much more grateful honesty exclaim: How odd it would have been had God not chosen the Jews! How wonderful, how fitting, and how gloriously beneficial to us has been that divine election of the Jewish people!

These are some of the things that could supply material for a sermon devoted to the topic of removing anti-Judaism from the pulpit. The particular selection of the material and the particular ways in which it is homiletically developed will vary greatly, depending on the context and the audience. All this must be left to the graced imagination of the preacher.

2. A second homiletic approach to removing anti-Judaism from the pulpit can be the sermon which, while devoted to another theme or occasion, seizes the opportunity offered by that occasion to give significant attention to this particular theme. To the homilist who is sensitive to this issue, numerous occasions will suggest themselves. In my own case, for example, the homily for a recent wedding provided just such an occasion. The bride and groom had chosen the following scriptural passages for the Liturgy of the Word: (1) Tobit 8:5–7 (the prayer of Tobiah and Sarah on their wedding night); (2) the Responsorial Psalm: "The Lord is kind and merciful"; (3) 1 Cor 12:31–13:8 (Paul's hymn to love); and (4) Jn 2:1–11 (the account of the miracle at the wedding feast of Cana.) Because I was preparing this wedding homily at the same time that I was doing some background reading for this essay, I was more than normally alert to issues of Judaism and anti-Judaism. Working in that context, I could not but make this issue a central theme of this wedding sermon. I did this by recounting briefly the plot of the beautiful and edifying book of Tobit written shortly before the time of Jesus. (It is part of the "Catholic" Bible; in the "Protestant" Bible, it is included among the apocrypha.) By way of illustration for this essay, I will quote the last major paragraph of that wedding homily:

> But woven into this story, holding it together from beginning to end—and this is apparently why it has become one of the sacred books—is a picture of the beauty and holiness of Jewish family life shortly before the time of Jesus: the fidelity, the concern, the love for one's spouse, one's children, one's parents, one's relatives, one's fellow human beings; a fidelity and loving service both in good times and in bad, whether rich or poor, whether in sickness or in health. All the essential elements of Christian family life and Christian social life are there, coming to us, live so to speak, from these final years of the so called Old Covenant (remember, it's really not "old," because it has never been revoked by God). We have here the sublime ideals of self giving, loving family life, one of the many great gifts of Judaism to the rest of the world. This was the kind of life,

the kind of feelings, the kind of attitudes that Mary and Joseph inculcated into their Son, Jesus. This was why Jesus groaned with compassion when he saw the poor, and the sick, and the blind. This was why he couldn't let the wine run out at the wedding feast at Cana—although it seems that he still needed some prodding from his mother on that score. And this Jewish life of loving concern was what enabled St. Paul to compose that magnificent hymn to love which we heard in the second reading which Mary Pat [the bride] proclaimed for us.

3. A third homiletic approach, one that can and should be used quite frequently, is the sermon which calls attention to this theme either by way of appropriate explanation or comment or as part of its general development. For example—a negative example—I recently heard a Sunday sermon delivered by a bright, young, homiletically talented Catholic priest. It was August 28, 1994, the twenty-second Sunday of the year in cycle B of the lectionary. The Gospel reading was from Mk 7:1–8, 14–15, 21–23 (Jesus' teaching about internal purity contrasted with merely external purity, a teaching occasioned by the Pharisees and scribes questioning why Jesus' disciples ate without first ritually washing their hands).

This is one of the controversy dialogues between Jesus and the scribes and Pharisees found frequently throughout the Gospels. It has the strong, if not indeed violent (to our sensibility) apologetic overtones characteristic of ancient polemic. It cries out for comment on several scores: (a) the contextualization of ancient apologetic so that the contemporary hearer would be reminded that in those days, this was the way in which even friends argued with each other; (b) the retrojection of late first-century Christian–Jewish bitterness back into the time of Christ, since this Gospel of Mark was written at a time when, sadly, Christians and Jews were beginning to experience each other less as brothers and friends and more as enemies; (c) some awareness of the critical role played by Jewish food laws and customs in inculcating a sense of the holiness of things, some awareness that the Christian sense of the sacramentality of material creation is one of Judaism's great gifts to Christianity, and so on. How disappointing that, in an otherwise excellent sermon, there was not the slightest suggestion of this! How easily it would have fit into and even supported the main themes of the sermon itself! But in terms of what was actually proclaimed from the pulpit that Sunday morning, the faithful could have gone from this sermon with erroneous supersessionist ideas strengthened rather than challenged, and with stereotypical ideas of Christian–Jewish opposition affirmed rather than corrected. Sadly, I am afraid, this situation is all too typical.

4. A fourth homiletic approach is one that I suggest should characterize practically every Christian sermon, or at least the preparation for every sermon. Thus I am not thinking here about sermons which are devoted to this theme, as in our first suggestion, nor about sermons which take up the occasion or opportunity to say something about this theme in the ways which I have indicated in my second and third suggestions. I am thinking rather about a tone or attitude that should characterize every Christian sermon, a tone or attitude that interprets and proclaims every biblical text in a way that reveals its positive Jewish presuppositions and content. It is a tone or attitude that one can develop by cultivating in oneself a kind of hermeneutic of suspicion, i.e., a suspicion that the general Christian audience will, at the least suggestion, and sometimes at no suggestion at all, interpret in a supersessionist way a whole range of New Testament texts, unless they are challenged to think otherwise, or unless their (often unconscious) supersessionist mentality is converted by positive references and allusions.

It is probably only on this level that the real solution will be found. Unfortunately, success on this level may also be the most difficult to achieve. It is not something that can be done just by deciding to do it. It is something that has to flow from the life and experiences and feelings of preachers who have in some way made their own, in subconscious affect as well as in conscious decision, a positive attitude toward Jews and Judaism. I suppose that what I am suggesting is that anti-Judaism will not completely disappear from the pulpit until all preachers of the Word have learned to love the Jews.

When Christian preachers know and love Judaism, they won't have to conscientize themselves in order to prepare for a special sermon against anti-Judaism, they won't have to make special efforts to direct an important part of a sermon or homily in this direction, they won't have to take thought how to contextualize or neutralize seemingly anti-Jewish passages in the New Testament. All this will happen naturally, and with that natural graciousness which Jeremiah spoke about when he heard the Lord say:

> *I will put my law within them, and I will write it upon their hearts; and I will be their God, and they shall by my people. And no longer shall each man teach his neighbor and each his brother, saying, "Know the Lord," for they shall all know me, from the least of them to the greatest, says the Lord (Jer 31:33–34).*

We Christians and Jews together firmly believe that that day will come. When it does, we know that it will be God's doing and not ours. But in this mysterious time of the "not yet," God seems to have left it largely to our efforts to do the things, including removing anti-Judaism from the pulpit, that will make real in our own lives at least something of the kingdom of peace, justice, and love which has been promised to us.

For Further Reading:

Charlesworth, James H., ed. *Jews and Christians: Exploring the Past, Present, and Future.* New York: The American Interfaith Institute/Crossroad, 1990.

Charlesworth, James H., ed. *Overcoming Fear Between Jews and Christians.* New York: The American Interfaith Institute/Crossroad, 1992.

Declaration on the Relationship of the Church to Non-Christian Religions (*Nostra aetate*). Walter M. Abbott, ed., *The Documents of Vatican II.* New York: America Press, 1966. Pp. 660–66 (see esp. no 4). Also in Austin Flannery, editor. *Vatican Council II: The Conciliar and Post Conciliar Documents.* Collegeville, Minn.: Liturgical Press, 1975. Pp. 738–42.

Efroymson, David P, Eugene J. Fisher and Leon Klenicki, eds. *Within Context: Essays on Jews and Judaism in the New Testament.* The American Interfaith Institute/Collegeville, Minn.: Glazier/Liturgical Press, 1993.

Evans, Craig A. and Donald A Hagner, editors. *Anti-Semitism and Early Christianity: Issues of Polemic and Faith.* Minneapolis: Fortress, 1993.

Lohfink, Norbert. *The Covenant Never Revoked: Biblical Reflections on Christian–Jewish Dialogue.* New York/ Mahwah, N.J., Paulist, 1991.

New Theology Review: An American Catholic Journal for Ministry. Vol. 7, No. 2 devoted to the theme: "The Church and the Jewish Tradition." Articles: Joseph A. Minding, O. F. M. Cap., "'Are They Hebrews? So Am I!': The Jewish Side of the Apostle to the Gentiles" pp. 6–17; James P. Scullion, O. F. M., "Pastoral Implications of a Jewish Jesus and a Jewish Paul" pp. 1–26; Hayim Goren Perelmuter, "Jesus the Jew: A Jewish Perspective" pp. 27–36.

CHAPTER SIX

Reflections of an Imported WASP

David H. C. Read

This chapter will be deliberately autobiographical, not because my experience as a Protestant preacher is unique, but because I'm sure that it isn't. There must be hundreds of us who, when confronted with the suggestion that there is anti-Judaism in our preaching, react with surprise mixed with indignation. It is perhaps only when we begin to reflect on the fact that the New Testament, which is the major source of our sermon texts, undoubtedly contains passages which seem to characterize the Jews as the enemies of Christians, that we have to ask ourselves if we have done anything in our exposition to repudiate what sounds at times like sheer anti-Semitism. (I remember when this point came home to me some years ago when I was in Yankee Stadium where a vast crowd—perhaps a majority Jewish—had assembled to hear a mass celebrated by the Pope. When the time came for the Gospel reading the first words we heard were from John's Gospel: "That evening, the doors being shut where the disciples were, for fear of the Jews. . . ." No further reference to these words was made, but I found myself for the first time hearing them as they might have sounded in Jewish ears.)

If Jews and Christians are going to understand one another better in these critical years of religious tensions when hopes of a new harmony are jostling with fears of a new fanaticism, we need more than ever to realize what lies behind our neighbor's faith (or lack thereof). This means our habit of pinning labels on people and thinking we have identified X, Y, and Z and know what to expect of them as Jews,

Catholics, Protestants or, it may be, Mormons, Zen Buddhists, Jehovah's Witnesses, or Bahais. When I once asked a few representatives of different faiths to come and speak to some of my own flock at Madison Avenue Presbyterian Church, I stressed that they were not being asked to defend their beliefs or to explain what seem to be its mysteries, but simply to tell us in their own words what it *feels* like to be a Moslim, a Baptist, a Quaker, or whatever, and why they were happy to remain one. Such a kind of opening-up can do much to reveal our common humanity without leading to popular fallacies like "We all believe in the same God" and "We're all going the same way." We don't, and we aren't. But with honesty and humility we can learn from one another.

Jews and Christians are, historically, more closely linked in beliefs and ethics than any other religions, and for that very reason have greater need for a serious effort towards mutual understanding. Rows "within the family" are reputed to be among the most violent, and the tragic history of relations between Jews and Christians is replete with not only ferocious debate and name calling, but explosions of hatred and persecution. For sensitive Christians the appalling climax of centuries of anti-Semitism (known to us as the Holocaust) compelled an agonizing re-appraisal of the Church's relation to the Jews and a fresh consideration of the subtle ways in which we may have been infected with the virus of popular anti-Semitism.

In that superb movie *Chariots of Fire*, two kinds of anti-Semitism came to the surface. Liddell, the young Scot who is totally devoted to his call to be a Christian missionary in China and whose religious principles, including the Ten Commandments, preclude his running an Olympic heat on "the Sabbath," is the center of interest. I sensed in the audience a surprising sympathy with this demonstration of what is often mocked as narrow-minded Calvinism, I realized there are many of our permissive generation who welcomed this example of a man willing to stand up to enormous social and even political pressure to conform, refusing to do what he believed to be wrong. What is also brilliantly portrayed are two kinds of anti-Judaism sparked by the fact that Liddell's rival on the college running track is Jewish. We are shown incidents of crude, popular anti-Judaism, but most impressive is the acceptable and "respectable" anti-Semitism of the WASP intellectual portrayed by the college dean played by John Gielgud. I was forced to wonder if I had been influenced by this bland and subtle anti-Judaism, or at least had tolerated it by my silence.

Yet this WASP was born and raised in Scotland which has no record of anti-Jewish legislation or forced expulsion of Jews. On the contrary, there has been since the Reformation a distinctly Jewish flavor in our popular theology and in the worship of the Church of Scotland, which is Presbyterian. What we called the Old Testament has loomed large in the religion of the average Scot. I recall hearing as many sermons based on the Old Testament as on the New; and in the public school system (thanks to John Knox, Scotland led Europe in the provision of a school for every parish in the land) every child was exposed to the Ten Commandments and the history of Israel with its stories of memorable characters as well as its songs and proverbs. To this day Scots literature contains many more such scriptural references than are to be found in English writers. The metrical version of the Twenty-third Psalm has become, over the years, almost a national anthem, to be sung spontaneously—along with the more secular "Scots wha hae." (The story goes that a scottish soldier was challenged by an English colleague who bet five shillings he couldn't recite the Lord's Prayer. "Done," said the Scot, beginning with the words "The Lord's my shepherd, I'll not want; he makes me down to lie; in pastures green. . . ." and so to the end of the metrical version of the psalm. The punch-line of the story is that the Englishman paid up, saying "I never thought you could do it!")

My secondary school in Edinburgh had about six hundred pupils, but I don't think there was one Jew among them. This had, I believe, nothing to do with anti-Jewish prejudice. My sister's school at that time had among its star pupils the son of Scotland's chief rabbi whom I later met in the English literature department of Edinburgh where he had a brilliant career, subsequently teaching both in England and the United States. Dr. David Daiches, whose books have a unique Scots–Jewish flavor, is now well known on both sides of the Atlantic as a scholar and a wit. (We were, of course, exposed occasionally to the typical anti-Jewish joke, but as these are usually the same jokes that are made about the Scots they were accepted as another

Scots-Jewish link rather than anti-Semitic barbs. There is a theory that accounts for the relatively small number of Jews by the fact they find it hard to make a living there!)

In the Bible hour at school, from which the few Roman Catholics were excused, we were not only exposed to the teaching and the stories of the Old Testament, but some attempt was made to explain Jewish devotion and ways of worship. (I remember how fascinated we were to hear that Jewish men kept their hats on in church!) We were told that Jesus was a Jew, but never once did I hear the accusation that Jews were Christ-killers and therefore accursed. Those who have been led to believe that all Christians are indoctrinated with this accusation may be surprised to hear that I never heard it until I went to Europe during my student years. Neither at home nor at school was this crude accusation of deicide part of my upbringing as a WASP. I mention this because from reports I have heard of synagogue sermons (often by Protestant organists who hear them regularly) I believe that sometimes there is serious misrepresentation of the average Protestant sermon.

What strikes me now as I look back at my theological training is not that we were taught to despise Judaism but that certain assumptions were too easily formed and that the major questions about the role of modern Judaism in God's providence were never confronted. Crudely speaking, we were left with the impression that the Jews were a wonderful people who "missed the boat" when Jesus came. From the evangelical point of view, they should be targeted for conversion; from the liberal, they were seen as "near Christian" with Unitarian convictions. From the time of my ordination and induction into my first parish in the border country of Scotland, I don't recall any presbytery meeting or informal discussion group where the question of the role of Judaism was discussed. This seems strange to me now as these were the year (1936–1940) when anti-Semitism had broken loose in Germany and Jewish refugees were by no means rare. Through my European contacts I had come to recognize the menace of anti-Semitism, but the average church member was more preoccupied with the avoidance of war than with the ideology of the Nazis.

As a Protestant preacher in New York I found myself in close contact with several rabbis and learned something of the life of modern Judaism, Orthodox, Conservative, and Reformed. I also learned from the experience of the few who became active members of our church, not for reasons of convenience but from profound religious conviction. I found myself very much in sympathy with the Vatican II's statement on evangelization of the Jews—including them in the welcome of the Gospel but recognizing that for many reasons that invitation is quite different from our approach to those of other religions. One of these resons is the appalling record of the Christian Church over the years. It has been said that over all our Judaeo–Christian dialogue and common social action there hangs the shadow of the Holocaust and the story of demonic anti-Semitism that produced it. My own change of attitude was deeply influenced by a renewed study of chapters nine to eleven of the Epistle to the Romans. I continue to find its agonizing over the question of the validity of the Old Testament in the light of the New both moving and enlightening.

It is this changed attitude that I try to pass on to WASP congregations. I don't mean that I have devoted many sermons to expounding Christian relationship to Judaism. Rather I have tried to instill an attitude of respect for the enduring faith of our "covenant cousins" in the God of Abraham and Sarah and of humility and hope as disciples of Christ. The Protestant pulpit should avoid the current trend to follow Gibbon's description of the cynical attitude of the late Roman empire when all religions were regarded by the faithful "as equally true, by the philosophers as equally false, and by the politicians as equally useful" and the policy of silence on the great questions that both link and divide Jews and Christians.

The Protestant preacher who would vigorously reject the accusation that his or her sermons were marked by a recognizable anti-Judaism has to ask a couple of disturbing questions: (1) Is my silence on the controversial issues that sometimes surface in the media concerning Jewish–Christian relations— evangelism, interfaith marriage, public recognition of respective religious festivals—not perhaps due to a reluctance to face genuine theological differences and thus rocking the delicately balanced boat of American religion? and (2) Have I been encouraging certain false assumptions and misrepresentations that have been part of the homiletical diet in a great many Protestant churches? There is, for instance, the simplistic picture of the Judaism of Jesus's contemporaries as a religion of harsh legalism dominated by a law whose regulations, ever expanding, were ruthlessly enforced by a kind of super-clergy known as Pharisees? This caricature of the Judaism that our Lord encountered has to be examined and exposed in such a way as to purge the Protestant pulpit of what is really an illiterate, if sincere anti-Judaism.

Most Protestants would, I believe, plead guilty to silence on some of the controversial issues in the multicultural, multi religious climate of our day. We seem to be afraid of anything that resonates with a clear, distinctive religious conviction lest it might offend our Jewish neighbors. My own belief is that Jewish–Christian dialogue can be fruitful only if each side is willing to confront the issues that divide, as well as those that unite us. I don't believe that we further good mutual understanding by sermons such as one I once read at Christmastime in which the preacher declared that Christmas and Chanukah celebrated almost identical events and conveyed almost the same message from God.

The other question forces us to realize that our preaching has been colored by a false picture of the religious climate in which Jesus was raised and in which he preached. The abundance of books about the Judaism of his day with its immense variety of beliefs and practices leaves us without excuse for having left our congregations with a distorted picture of a Jesus who appeared suddenly from the supernatural world with a message of God's love and grace which appealed to the poor and oppressed but who was crushed by the harsh theology of the religious leaders and their political allies. The numerous studies that have appeared concerning "the Jewishness of Jesus" and the impact of cults like the Essenes of the Dead Sea Scrolls are surely being read by preachers, but little of their content has appeared in the pulpit. Worshipers have been left with the impression, for instance, that the Pharisees were the representatives of a religion of law, of strict observance of a multitude of awkward and petty requirements, and devoid of the qualities of mercy and love. A closer examination of New Testament texts reveals a different picture. Sermons could reflect not only the often quoted statement that "The Law was given by Moses, but grace and truth came by Jesus Christ," but also the words of Jesus: "Do not think that I have come to abolish the law or the prophets; I have not come to abolish but to fulfill" (Matt. 5:17).

This assumption that the Pharisees are representatives of hard, unbending legalism ties in with an impression left by many of our sermons that Judaism ceased to be a living faith with the emergence of the Christian Church. Reflecting on my own experience, I find that seminary training did little to awaken me to the spiritual content of the voluminous literature of Judaism both before and after the Christian era. I remember in my early days as a preacher being forced to reconsider the assumption that the New Testament gospel of God's grace had replaced the Law as the center of a living religion and therefore presumably rendered most of the Old Testament obsolete. I realized that the old covenant still had a prominent place in the confessions and the worship of the Reformed Church. As such I was obligated to preach from many of its texts. But how? I found in sermon preparation that, for instance, there was a Hebrew word (*chesed*) which referred to what Christians meant by grace. It used to be translated by the words "mercy" or "loving-kindness" and abounded in the Book of Psalms. (Modern translations have generally replaced "loving-kindness" with "steadfast love" which may be more accurate but is surely less euphonious.) Thanks to scholars like Martin Buber, Rayond Brown, Frederick Neuman, George Landes, and many others from different theological perspectives, I began to treat the Old Testament as something much more than a repository of texts that could be used (or twisted) into literal prophecies of Jesus. I discovered some of the spiritual riches of a living Judaism as reflected in the Talmudic and other traditions through centuries of Jewish and Christian coexistence.

If, then, other Christian preachers share something of my experience, my plea for this is threefold: (1) that we bring our reading and thinking about the relationship of the two covenants up-to-date; (2) that we strive to convey the results of this reading and thinking in our preaching and leading of worship and bible studies; and (3) that we foster dialogue which is based on mutual respect and search, but which does not inhibit either Jew or Christian from a frank recognition and expression of their deepest convictions.

CHAPTER SEVEN

Preaching the Gospel without Anti-Judaism

Fredrick C. Holmgren

"When are we going to take the Bible seriously? Our kids are still babies when it comes to knowing Scripture," a church member commented during a discussion of youth programming. True, in some respects we have done a poor job of making our congregations biblically literate. But at the same time, we have been all too successful in handing down some of the church's misunderstandings of Scripture's teachings. One need think only of the way that many Christians have used the Bible to keep African–Americans as second class citizens, to hold women in subjection to men, and to mark Jews as rejected by God. This "knowledge" of Scripture has been taught clearly and publicly—and passed on so effectively that for generations blacks, women, and Jews were kept "in their place."

Change is coming about; certainly public speech has changed. Racist, sexist, and anti-Semitic expressions are heard far less often. Yet destructive caricatures are still alive in private thoughts that keep us silent when we should be speaking firmly against these injustices.

Over the past twenty years, I have offered at a Midwest seminary a course in "Jews, Christians, and the Bible." Often I have found that people who pull back from overt anti-Judaism never the less harbor a latent version because of the teaching they have received within the church. This anti-Judaism is fueled by the fact that most Jews did not and do

From *The Christian Ministry*p, May–June, 1995.

not "accept" Christ. But that cannot be the only reason, since the majority of the world's people have not "accepted" Christ and yet Christians do not hold them to similarly harsh judgment. The reasons for anti-Judaism may be many, but the kinship and competition between Judaism and Christianity plays an important part; it has created "attack" language. This kind of language is prominent in the traditional Christian interpretation of the Jewish Scripture (the Old Testament) and is reflected in false portrayals of Jews and Judaism. The following are three common misrepresentations.

Misconception One: Israelites/Jews are an exceptionally rebellious people

Embedded in the Hebrew Bible are many fierce—even savage—denunciations of the Israelites. Isaiah calls them a "sinful nation, laden with iniquity," "who have despised" God, and "who are utterly estranged" (1:4). Jeremiah questions whether it is possible to find in Jerusalem even "one person who acts justly and seeks truth" (5:1), and Ezra declares in prayer that "our [Jewish] iniquities have risen higher than our heads, and our guilt has mounted up to the heavens" (9:6). If these words are to be taken literally, then the church fathers were right when they spoke of the Israelites (and Jews) as a people who were extraordinary sinners. Were the Israelites that sinful? Certainly nowhere else in the ancient Near East do prophets so severely denounce their own communities. Are we to believe that of all the peoples in the ancient world, the Israelites were the worst?

Scholars of ancient Near Eastern cultures indicate that the evidence points in the opposite direction: *no people in the ancient world were more self-critical—more sensitive to the wrongs of their society—than the Israelites*. The fact that this society did not suppress the uncompromising prophetic voice (although some prophets were persecuted and killed) witnesses to a community whose heart remained open to divine censure. Further, the existence of the prophets assumes the presence of other faithful people who shared their views (see 1 Kings 19:18 and 20:15). Although these prophetic denunciations are to be taken seriously, they do not mean that Jews were more sinful than other people. That such texts from the Hebrew Bible are part of our lectionary today makes us aware that the sins attacked by ancient prophets and reformers are still present within the Christian community.

It is remarkable that these prophetic denunciations survived to become part of our reading today. These accusatory passages were not forgotten or destroyed but preserved by the Jewish community itself, who set them apart as Holy Scripture. Such a people should not be accused of continuing rebellion against God. There were serious problems in ancient Hebrew society; Christian preachers, as do rabbis, may refer to the sins committed within the Israelite community. But in so doing they should underscore that this aspect of the Bible mirrors the evil that afflicts every society—including the Christian community.

Misconception Two: Jews do not believe the predictions of their own Scriptures

A traditional Christian approach to the relationship between the Hebrew and Christian Scriptures has been to speak of the former as "promise/prediction" and the latter as "fulfillment." Jews have suffered under this interpretation because they have been depicted as rebellious sinners who have defiantly shut their eyes to the obvious predictions of Jesus in the Jewish Bible. Many contemporary Christian biblical scholars call attention to the misrepresentation created by such a view of the Hebrew Scriptures. John Goldingay, for example, observes that there is no clear reference to Jesus in the Jewish Bible. He declares: "It is not self-evident that Christ is the fulfillment of OT [Old Testament] hopes. Whether one recognizes him as such will be dependent on whether one is willing to acknowledge him for his own sake" (*Approaches to Old Testament Interpretation*, InterVarsity [1981], p. 119).

How, then, did the early Christians "find" Jesus in the Jewish Bible, if there were no definite and clear predictions concerning him? In this brief chapter, I am unable to discuss completely the varied ways in which the New Testament authors used the Old Testament; therefore, I will limit the discussion to some passages that use the term "fulfill." This term appears about twenty-five times in the Christian Scriptures and has a nuanced range of meanings. When these meanings are considered one finds it difficult to speak about direct New Testament fulfillments of Old Testament predictions—predictions that precede the rise of Christianity by many centuries.

Rather, within these New Testament passages, one finds that "fulfill" has the sense of "is similar to" or "analogous to" an earlier event recorded in the Old Testament. The idea appears to be that the earlier event is, in some similar form, happening again and in this sense is "fulfilled." With the insight provided by faith in Christ, early Christians were persuaded that the New Testament events confirmed and deepened the Old Testament witness that God is at work in our world.

An example of a New Testament author quoting an Old Testament passage because it seemed similar to what happened to Jesus is the citation of Hos. 11:1 in Matt. 2:15. Hosea recalls the divine intervention on behalf of the Hebrews in Egypt when God brought Israel (God's child) out of Egypt (cf. also Exod. 4:22–23). Matthew, writing some seven hundred years later than Hosea, speaks of the time when Mary, Joseph, and the infant Jesus were returning from Egypt to Israel after the death of Herod. Matthew declares: "This was to fulfill what had been spoken by the Lord through the prophet, 'Out of Egypt I have called my son.'" The use of the term "fulfill" does not intend to convey an exact fulfillment of a seven-hundred-year-old prediction. Almost every biblical scholar agrees that Hosea is referring to the nation Israel. There is no direct, explicit reference to Jesus. Rather the Gospel writer believes that this ancient text points to and is similar to God's act in bringing Jesus back from Egypt after the death of Herod. This divine deliverance of Jesus and his family testifies that the God of the Exodus continues to preserve his people.

One more example of an analogical relationship between an Old and New Testament text is the citation of Ps. 41:9 in John 13:18. In the latter passage, Jesus is speaking of his betrayal and in so doing declares: "But it is to fulfill the Scripture, 'The one who ate my bread has lifted his heel against me.'" The passage in Psalm 41 is not a direct prediction of this betrayal. Instead of providing a sharp focus on Jesus and Judas, the psalmist is speaking about a painful, recurring experience that a great number of people know all too well: the experience of being betrayed by a friend. This tragic experience is part of proverbial wisdom both in Israel (Prov. 27:6: "Profuse are the kisses of an enemy") and Egypt ("It was he who ate my food that raised up troops against me and he to whom I had given my hands that created terror thereby," The Instruction of King

Amen-em-het, lines 20–22). Jesus' experience of what was taking place in his own inner circle reminded the Gospel writer of the hurt of the psalmist who was cut down by the pretense of friendship and loyalty.

A final example may be found in the use that Matt. 2:16–18 makes of Jer. 31:15. The Gospel writer has in mind Herod's murder of the Jewish children when he announces, "Then was fulfilled what had been spoken through the prophet Jeremiah: 'A voice was heard in Ramah, wailing and loud lamentation, Rachel weeping for her children; she refused to be consoled because they are no more.'" Jeremiah refers to the hopeless situation of the Israelites who were suffering exile in the environs of Babylon. To understand the text one needs to remember that Jacob and Rachel are regarded as the nation's parents. Mother Rachel weeps over the suffering of her children in a foreign land. Herod's slaughter of the children reminded Matthew of this similar event recorded in Jeremiah. A sermon on this text should deal not simply with the tragic events of the past, but also remind us that the Jeremiah passage has been fulfilled again and again. Rachel has cried many times through the centuries as her children have been persecuted and killed.

Misconception Three: The Old Testament is antiquated

The Christian church received the Scriptures from the Jewish community, and the only Bible that first-century Christians used was the Jewish Scriptures. The traditional Christian title, "Old Testament," makes some good sense because it is older than the Scripture that arose out of the Christian movement. The word "old," however, is susceptible to another meaning, namely, "antiquated." Some New Testament texts point to such a view of the Old Testament by saying that the covenant that God made through Moses is "obsolete" (Heb. 8:13). Although few Christians today would speak in such strong, negative terms about the Old Testament, many view this Jewish Bible as an ancient, out-of-date, second-level Scripture that the church does not really need. Its basic value, it is thought, is that it points to the New Testament.

But, of course, this "old, second level" Scripture is the only canonical Scripture of Judaism; therefore, Judaism is judged to be an inadequate religion. Even though Judaism is not simply the religion of the Old Testament but has, like Christianity, grown out of and beyond the context of this Scripture, it is still tagged as an "Old Testament kind of faith" and therefore judged deficient. A full knowledge of Judaism will quickly dispel that judgment; however, in the following paragraphs I will not focus on Judaism, but on the Hebrew Bible/Old Testament.

What is the character of this Scripture that has nourished the Jewish community through long and difficult centuries? What does it contribute to the New Testament and to Christianity? Increasingly we are recognizing that the Old Testament brings gifts to the Christian tradition. One of those gifts is the Torah (the Law). The Old Testament and the Jewish tradition know, of course, that some people can distort Torah and make it something other than it is (as happens also with the teaching of grace in Christian circles), but without the Torah Christianity would have a different character.

Jesus embraced the Torah of Moses; he came not to end it but to fulfill it (Matt. 5:17)—to carry its teachings forward. Further, to those who came to him seeking eternal life, he held it up as the essential teaching to be observed (Luke 10:25–28). Despite Jesus' conflict with some interpreters of his day, both Jewish and Christian scholars see him as one who honored and followed the Law. When Jesus proclaims the coming rule of God, he speaks nowhere in detail about the inner character of this rule. He does not need to because that has already been described in the Old Testament and spoken of in Judaism. The realm of God follows the path of justice and kindness taught in Torah.

Some Christian scholars (at the suggestion of Herbert Haag and Erich Zenger) have used the term "plus" to describe the Old Testament's gifts to the New Testament. One such plus is the Old Testament's concern about everyday matters. Although this concern is not absent in the New Testament, the older Scripture emphasizes it much more strongly. Whereas the New Testament, in its focus on Jesus Christ, holds before us the ideal life we should live, the Old Testament speaks to our daily experiences in this world, to our hopes, pain, sin, forgiveness, anger, violence, despair, joy, doubts, and relationships with others. The fact that the book of Psalms has often been printed with the New Testament underscores that the New Testament needs to be supplemented with this ancient book's depiction of the diversity of life experiences. It is especially in the Old Testament that we hear of a God who accepts and listens to us as we speak our raw thoughts. The New Testament contains nothing like the book of Job or the psalms of lament, which voice questions and complaints to the Almighty.

The church needs the Old Testament emphasis on a God who fully understands and accepts us as we confront this world— who is aware that everyday life is complex and often hard and who, despite our frailty, respects our integrity and does not dismiss our complaints and questions as unimportant. Further, the Old Testament's strong dual emphasis on God's concern for this world and our responsibility in it (see Exodus and the Prophets) stands as an important check on the church's constant temptation to focus on personal, spiritual salvation and life after death. Perhaps it is this special emphasis—this "plus"—in the Old Testament that makes it so attractive to many Christian communities in the newly emerging nations. The God witnessed to in this part of the Christian canon understands well the cries arising from the oppressed.

The Old Testament is not an antiquated Scripture; its life-giving teachings are needed by the church. Pastors can help impart a more respectful attitude toward it by using other titles, such as "the Scripture," "the Bible" or the "First Testament." Also, in order to indicate that the church has received this book of life from Judaism, one can at times use the terms "the Hebrew Bible" or "the Jewish Bible." The adoption of such expressions would be a way of extending thankfulness to the Jewish community for preserving these books for those of us who are among the later born. In church bulletins, instead of calling the readings Old and New Testament Scriptures, why not use "The Scripture: Psalm 51; The Scripture: Luke 5:17–26." And finally, in the liturgy, we sometimes should read the New Testament text first and the Old Testament second. Our choice of words and actions communicates our thinking and helps shape opinion within the congregation. In these simple ways—without compromising our commitment to Christ—we can do much to bring about a fair and generous understanding of the Old Testament and Judaism.

For Further Reading

Charlesworth, James, ed. *Jesus' Jewishness: Exploring the Place of Jesus within Early Judaism.* Crossroad, 1991.

Charlesworth, James and W. P. Weaver, eds. *The Old and New Testaments: Their Relationship and the "Intertestamental" Literature.* Trinity, 1993.

Lapide, Pinchas and Ulrich Luz. *Jesus in Two Perspectives: A Jewish–Christian Dialog.* Augsburg, 1985.

Lohfink, Norbert. *The Covenant Never Revoked: Biblical Reflections on Christian–Jewish Dialogue.* Paulist, 1991.

Williamson, Clark M. and Ronald J. Allen. *Interpreting Difficult Texts: Anti-Judaism and Christian Preaching.* Trinity, 1989.

CHAPTER EIGHT

Preaching Jews and Judaism in Light of the New Catechism

Peter C. Phan

Promulgated by Pope John Paul II on October 11, 1992, *Catechism of the Catholic Church* has been a best seller in many countries.[1] Six years in the making, the eight-hundred-page work has received both enthusiastic encomium and harsh criticism.[2] However one judges its merits, undeniably *Catechism*, if used as intended, will shape the Roman Catholic tradition for a long time to come. It stands to reason, then, that part of the effort to eradicate anti-Semitism from Roman Catholic preaching must include an examination of the *Catechism's* presentation of Jews and Judaism.

I. The *Catechism* on Jews and Judaism

The first thing to notice is that, whereas Vatican ll presents Judaism most thoroughly in the context of non-Christian

---

1. The original language of the text is French, published as *Catéchisme de l'Eglise Catholique* (Paris: Mame – Librairie Editrice Vaticane, 1992). Its *editio typica*, however, is in Latin. The English translation was published in June 1994. Because of the exclusive language of the official English version, I will not use it but rather provide my own translation based on the French original.
2. For a short history of the composition of the *Catechism*, see Joseph Ratzinger, "Progress Report on the Universal *Catechism*," *The Living Light* 27/1 (1991): 131–38 and William J. Levada, "The *Catechism* for the Universal Church," *The Living Light* 26/3 (1990): 199–209. For a bibliography on the project of composing a universal *catechism* and on its draft, see Thomas J. Reese, "Bibliographical Survey on the *Catechism* for the Universal Church," *The Living Light* 27/3 (1991): 151–57. For a critical but balanced introduction to the *Catechism*, see *Introducing the Catechism of the Catholic Church: Traditional Themes and Contemporary Issues*, ed. Berard Marthaler (New York: Paulist Press, 1994).

religions, Catechism intentionally avoids such an approach.[3] Instead, it adopts the scheme of Vatican II's constitution on the church which speaks of the various ways in which different people are related to the church in their search for God.[4] Jews, then, are placed in the category of "those who have not yet received the Gospel" and are said to be "related to the People of God in various ways" (no. 839).[5]

In comparison with Vatican II, however, *Catechism* makes two new points. First, in contemporary Catholic theology there is a debate as to whether non-Christian religions are merely the fruit of the human search for God or have already participated in divine revelation. *Catechism* declines to settle the issue on the ground that the magisterium has not made a sufficiently clear pronouncement on the matter.[6] However, it recognizes the special position of Judaism vis-a-vis other non-Christian religions: "The Jewish faith, unlike other non-Christian religions, is already a response to God's revelation in the Old Testament" (no. 839). In describing the various stages of God's self-revelation in an earlier chapter on God's coming to meet humanity, *Catechism* speaks of God's self-communication to the first parents, to Noah, and to Abraham: "The people descended from Abraham would be the trustees of the promise made to the patriarchs, the chosen people, called to prepare for that day when God would gather all his children into the unity of the church" (no. 60). Clearly, then, whatever opinion one holds about the revelatory character of other religions, doubt cannot be entertained that God has been *revealed* in Judaism. Christian theologians must be mindful of the unique position of Judaism as a revealed religion.

Secondly, *Catechism* explicitly raises the issue of the Messiah and points out the difference in the expectation of the Messiah among Christians and Jews:

3. See Vatican II *Declaration on the Relation of the Church to Non-Christian Religions (Nostra Aetate)*. The declaration briefly describes, with increasing length, Hinduism, Buddhism, Islam, and Judaism.

4. See *Lumen Gentium*, no. 16. Choosing the words carefully, the document speaks of Roman Catholics as "fully incorporated" into the church, non-Catholic Christians as "joined" to the church, and non-Christians as "related" to the church.

5. Citations from Catechism will be indicated in parentheses in the body of the essay by giving the number of the paragraph, not the page of the book.

6. See Joseph Ratzinger, "Progress Report on the Universal Catechism," *The Living Light* 27/3 (1991): 136.

And when one considers the future, God's People of the Old Covenant and the New People of God tend toward similar goals: expectation of the coming (or the return) of the Messiah. But one awaits the return of the Messiah who died and rose from the dead and is recognized as Lord and Son of God; the other awaits the coming of a Messiah, whose features remain hidden till the end of time; and the latter waiting is accompanied by the drama of not knowing or of misunderstanding Christ Jesus (no. 840).

This common, though distinct, expectation of the Messiah constitutes an important ground for doctrinal dialogue and practical collaboration between adherents of these two religions.

Mention of the Messiah brings us to consider how *Catechism* regards the relationship between what it calls the "Old Testament" and the "New Testament" and the connected question of how to interpret the Old Testament.[7] The First Testament, *Catechism* declares, "is an indispensable part of Sacred Scripture. Its books are divinely inspired and retain a permanent value, for the Old Testament has never been revoked" (no. 121). With regard to the interpretation of the Scripture, *Catechism* stresses the importance of discerning the "literal meaning" of a text conveyed by the human authors in their words (nos. 109–16). But it also recognizes the necessity of going beyond the literal sense of the bible to discover its "spiritual sense," dividing the latter, according to an ancient usage, into allegorical, moral, and analogical senses (nos. 116–18).

7. For an informative and balanced study of the teaching of *Catechism* on biblical hermeneutics, see Joseph Jensen, "Beyond the Literal Sense: The Interpretation of Scripture in the *Catechism of the Catholic Church*," *The Living Light* 29/4 (1993): 50–60. With regard to the term "Old Testament" Jensen argues persuasively that what is referred to as the "Old Testament" in the Christian Scripture is not identical with the "Hebrew Scripture" in terms of both its contents and the order in which its books are arranged. He also agrees with Lawrence Boadt that alternative terms such as "The First Testament" and "The Prime Testament" run the risk of reading of the Bible in a disjunctive way rather than from the final viewpoint of the New Testament. He is careful to point out, however, that the use of the term "Old Testament" should not suggest that God's covenant with Israel is no longer valid or superceded. Even with this caveat, it is often the case among average Christians that the term "Old Testament," given the long history of the Christian "teaching of contempt" against Jews, conveys obsoleteness and supersession. For this reason I will use "First Testament" and "Second Testament" when speaking for myself and "Old Testament" and "New Testament" when quoting *Catechism*.

More specifically, in interpreting the First Testament, Catechism affirms the legitimacy of the typological approach prevalent before the advent of the historical critical method. Typology, it argues, is justified by the unity between the two Testaments, provided that the continuing efficacy and validity of the First Testament is maintained: "Christians therefore read the Old Testament in the light of Christ crucified and risen. Such typological reading discloses the inexhaustible content of the Old Testament; but it must not make us forget that the Old Testament retains its own intrinsic value as revelation reaffirmed by our Lord himself. Besides, the New Testament has to be read in the light of the Old" (no. 129).

This typological approach or the promise–fulfillment scheme also governs *Catechism's* understanding of the church's liturgical worship: "In the sacramental economy the Holy Spirit fulfills what was prefigured in *the Old Covenant*" (no. 1093). Fulfillment, however, does not imply abolition; on the contrary, *Catechism* says, the church's liturgy has retained elements of the worship of the Old Covenant as "integral and irreplaceable" (no. 1093), adopting them as its own. Such elements include reading the First Testament, praying the Psalms, and recalling the saving events and significant realities of the Jewish history. *Catechism* urges that catechesis unveil "what lay hidden under the letter of the Old Testament: the mystery of Christ" (no. 1094). This catechesis is called "typological" because "it reveals the newness of Christ on the basis of the 'figures' (types) which announce in the deeds, words, and symbols of the first covenant" (no. 1094). Catechesis should not, however, look only toward the past. Interestingly, *Catechism* affirms that "a better knowledge of the Jewish people's faith and religious life *as professed and lived even now* can help our better understanding of certain aspects of Christian liturgy" (no. 1096).[8]

The typological approach is also operative in *Catechism's* understanding of the relationship between what it calls "the Old Law" and "the New Law or the Law of the Gospel." It

8. Italics added. The italicized part seems to be a quotation from John Paul II's March 6, 1982 speech to the delegates of episcopal conferences and other experts meeting in Rome to study relations between the church and Judaism, though reference to it is not given. Regrettably, *Catechism* does not follow its own counsel when it comes to expound Christian worship and prayer.

acknowledges that God has revealed his law to Israel and that the "Law of Moses," summed up in the Ten Commandments, is "holy, spiritual, and good." Nevertheless, it is "still imperfect": "Like a tutor it shows what must be done, but does not of itself give the strength, the grace of the Spirit, to fulfill it. Because of sin, which it cannot remove, it remains a law of bondage" (no. 1963). Again here typology predominates: "The Old Law is *a preparation for the Gospel*. . . . It prophesies and presages the work of liberation from sin which will be fulfilled in Christ: it provides the New Testament with images, 'types,' and symbols for expressing the life according to the Spirit" (no. 1964). Concerning the sabbath, for example, which is said to be "at the heart of Israel's law" (no. 348), *Catechism* declares that for Christians the ceremonial observance of Sunday, which is "the eighth day" (no. 349), "replaces that of the sabbath" (no. 2175).

In sum, in its exposition of the relationship between Judaism and the church, *Catechism's* basic metaphor is that of promise–fulfillment, preparation–consummation, foretelling–realization: "The remote *preparation* for this gathering together of the People of God begins when God calls Abraham and promises that he will become the father of a great people. Its immediate preparation begins with Israel's election as the People of God. By this election, Israel is to be the sign of the future gathering of all nations. But the prophets also accuse Israel of breaking the covenant and behaving like a prostitute. They announce a new and eternal covenant. Christ instituted this covenant'" (no. 762).

Jesus and the Jews

One of the central themes in Jewish–Christian dialogue is the relationship of Jesus to the Law and to the Jews of his time, both in his public ministry and at his death. *Catechism* speaks of Jesus as "the only one who could keep it (the Law) perfectly" (no. 578), as the one who "did not abolish the Law but fulfilled it by giving its ultimate interpretation in a divine way" (no. 581). Furthermore, according to *Catechism*, Jesus has the deepest respect for the Temple, was willing to pay the Temple tax, and even "identified himself with the Temple by presenting himself as God's definitive dwelling place among humanity" (no. 586). Nevertheless, Jesus' attitude toward the Law and the Temple scandalized the Pharisees and the Sadducees. Of the Pharisees, *Catechism* says: "This principle of integral observance of the Law not only in the letter but in spirit was dear to the Pharisees. By giving Israel this principle they had led many Jews of Jesus' time to an extreme religious zeal. This zeal, were it not to lapse into 'hypocritical' casuistry, could only prepare the People for the unprecedented intervention of God through the perfect fulfillment of the Law by the only Righteous One in place of all sinners" (no. 579).[9]

According to *Catechism*, Jesus asked the "religious authorities" of Jerusalem to believe in him; but such an act of faith demands "a mysterious death to self" (no. 591). It is understandable, then, *Catechism* goes on to say, that they refused Jesus' demand and "judged that he deserved the death sentence as a blasphemer. The members of the Sanhedrin were thus acting at the same time out of 'ignorance' and the 'hardness' of their 'unbelief'" (no. 591).

With regard to Jesus' trial, *Catechism* notes the division of opinion among "the Jewish authorities." But it makes it clear that "the Sanhedrin, having declared Jesus deserving of death as a blasphemer but having lost the right to put anyone to death, hands him over to the Romans, accusing him of political revolt. . . . The high priests also threatened Pilate politically so that he would condemn Jesus to death" (no. 596).

Judaism and Prayer

The last part of *Catechism*, which deals with prayer, offers profound insights on prayer in Judaism. Viewing prayer as "a reciprocal call, a covenant drama" (no. 2567) between God and humanity, God searching for and responding to humans

---

9. This text is quite ambiguous: on the one hand, *Catechism* praises the Pharisees for their "principle of integral observance"; on the other hand, this principle is said to have led many Jews to "extreme religious zeal" which turned into "hypocritical casuistry" (reference is made to Mt 15:3–7 and Lk 11:39–54). In fact, the text did not explicitly say that the Pharisees' "extreme religious zeal" de facto turned into "hypocritical casuistry." Rather it says circuitously that this zeal could have prepared people to welcome Jesus if it "did not wish to turn itself into a hypocritical casuistry." The French text reads: "Celui-ci (i.e., extreme religious zeal), s'il ne voulait pas se résoudre en une casuistique 'hypocrite', ne pouvait que préparer le Peuple à cette intervention de Dieu inouïe que sera l'exécution parfaite de la Loi par le seul Juste à la place de tous les pécheurs."

and humans responding to and searching for God, *Catechism* describes Jewish prayer by locating it in the history of the Jewish people. With a deft touch and a sure sense of synthesis, it presents the various forms of Jewish prayer beginning with Abraham and ending with the psalter.

In Abraham's "attentiveness of the heart" (no. 2570) to God's word, *Catechism* sees the essence of prayer, and in his obedience to God's command to sacrifice his only son, it sees "the father of believers . . . conformed to the likeness of the Father who will not spare his own Son but will deliver him up for all" (no. 2572). In Jacob's night-long wrestling with a mysterious figure, it acknowledges the symbol of prayer as "a battle of faith and as the triumph of perseverance" (no. 2573). The prayer of Moses is "the most striking example of intercessory prayer" (no. 2574) and his experience of the burning bush is "one of the primordial images of prayer in the spiritual tradition of Jews and Christians alike" (no. 2575). David is proclaimed as "the first prophet of Jewish and Christian prayer" (no. 2579). The Temple is for the Jewish people "the place of their education in prayer: pilgrimages, feasts, and sacrifices, the evening offering, the incense, and the bread of the Presence ("shrewbread")—all these signs of the holiness and glory of God Most High and Most Near were appeals and ways of prayer" (no. 2581). However, because "ritualism often encouraged an excessively external worship" (no. 2581), the prophets, in particular Elijah, were commissioned by God to educate their people in "faith and conversion of heart" (no. 2581). Finally, the psalms, "the masterwork of prayer in the Old Testament" (no. 2585), "both nourished and expressed the prayer of the People of God gathered during the great feasts at Jerusalem and each Sabbath in the synagogues. . . . Prayed by Christ and fulfilled in him, the Psalms remain essential to the prayer of the Church" (no. 2586).

The final line of the last quotation reveals both the strength and weakness of *Catechism's* treatment of Jewish prayer. On the one hand, it recognizes Jewish prayer, especially the psalms, as an essential and permanent element of Christian prayer. On the other hand, following its typological approach, *Catechism* sees it primarily as foreshadowing and announcing the prayers of Christ and the church. Every Jewish master of prayer, from Abraham to Moses to David to Elijah, is viewed principally as a type of Christ whose practice of and teaching on prayer fulfilled all Jewish prayers.

Jesus as the Hope of Israel

It was pointed out above how *Catechism* views Jews and Christians as having a similar goal, i.e., the expectation of the coming or return of the Messiah whose "features remain hidden till the end of time" for Jews, and how this expectation of the Jews is "accompanied by the drama of not knowing or of misunderstanding Jesus" (no. 840). In its exposition of the glorious return of Jesus, *Catechism* repeats Paul's teaching on the "conversion" of all Israel as the condition for Jesus' *parousia*, without however explaining how it will come about:

> The glorious Messiah's coming is suspended at every moment of history until his recognition by "all Israel," for "a hardening has come upon part of Israel" in their "unbelief" toward
> Jesus. . . . The "full inclusion" of the Jews in the Messiah's salvation, in the wake of "the full number of the Gentiles" will enable the People of God to achieve "the measure of the stature of the fullness of Christ," in which "God may be all in all" (no. 674).

Because *Catechism* does not proffer any exegesis of Romans 9–11, it is not clear what it means by "the 'full inclusion' of the Jews in the Messiah's salvation." It may leave the impression that all Jews will somehow join the church and become Christians, which is far from what Paul had in mind.[10]

II. *Catechism* in Light of Earlier Ecclesiastical Documents

Commentators on *Catechism* have noted the extraordinarily large amount of quotations from a variety of sources that are often strung together in its text. It is all the more surprising then that in discussing Judaism and its relationship to Christianity it fails to make use of earlier ground-breaking

---

10. For a helpful interpretation of Romans 9–11, see Sidney G. Hall III, *Christian Anti-Semitism and Paul's Theology* (Minneapolis: Fortress, 1993), 113–27. Hall argues that Paul did not demand of the Jews that they "accept Christ" and hence become Christians but that they accept "the gospel of Christ," namely, the inclusive claim that Gentiles are beloved children of Abraham outside the Law.

ecclesiastical documents, except for an abbreviated citation from *Nostra Aetate*.[11] It is also regrettable that in its condemnation of discrimination it does not cite the only text of Vatican II that explicitly rejects anti-Semitism: "The church repudiates all persecutions against any human being. Moreover, mindful of its common patrimony with the Jews, and motivated by the gospel's spiritual love and by no political considerations, it deplores the hatred, persecutions, and displays of anti-Semitism directed against the Jews at any time and from any source."[12]

Among Roman documents on the relationship between Judaism and Christianity with which *Catechism* should be compared and contrasted, two obtain pride of place: *Guidelines and Suggestions for Implementing the Conciliar Declaration Nostra Aetate* (4) [December 1, 1974] and *Notes on the Correct Way to Present the Jews and Judaism in Preaching and Catechesis in the Roman Catholic Church* [June 24, 1985], both issued by the Vatican Commission for Religious Relations with the Jews.[13]

A comparison between *Catechism* on the one hand and *Guidelines* and *Notes* on the other will show that the former represents an unfortunate step backward in the understanding of

---

11. The citation is taken from paragraph 4: ..."[N]either all Jews indiscriminately at that time, nor Jews today, can be charged with the crimes committed during his Passion.... [T]he Jews should not be spoken of as rejected or accursed as if this followed from holy Scripture." It is somewhat strange that in a book purported to be the standard for catechetical instruction and preaching, the rest of the paragraph is omitted: "All should take pains, then, lest in catechetical instruction and in the preaching of God's Word they teach anything out of harmony with the truth of the gospel and the spirit of Christ."

12. *Nostra Aetate*, no. 4. *Catechism* deals with discrimination in nos. 1934–1938. In condemning discrimination it cites *Gaudium et Spes*, no. 29, #2: "Every form of social or cultural discrimination in fundamental personal rights on the grounds of sex, race, color, social conditions, language, or religion, must be curbed and eradicated as incompatible with God's design."

13. The English texts are available in *In Our Time: The Flowering of Jewish–Catholic Dialogue*, ed. Eugene Fisher and Leon Klenicki (New York: Paulist Press, 1990), pp. 29–50.

The first document will be referred to as *Guidelines*, the second as *Notes*. The pages refer to those of this book. Fisher provides an introduction to these two documents, Klenicki a critical evaluation of them.

Another document, titled *Within Context: Guidelines for the Catechetical Presentation of Jews and Judaism in the New Testament* (1986), is of great importance for our theme. It is not issued by the Vatican but was prepared in collaboration by the Secretariat for Catholic–Jewish Relations of the National Conference of Catholic Bishops, the Education Department of the United States Catholic Conference, and Interfaith Affairs Department of the Anti-Defamation League of B'nai B'rith. The text is also available in the volume *In Our Time*, pp. 59–74, and will be referred to as *Within Context*.

the relationship between Judaism and Christianity. I will highlight some areas in which this regression occurs.

1. We have seen how in the area of hermeneutics *Catechism's* approach is predominantly typological.[14] Despite its caveat that the First Testament books "retain a permanent value, for the Old Covenant has never been revoked" (no. 121) and that the literal sense, discovered by means of the historical–critical method, is primary, *Catechism* has made little effort to understand the original meaning of the First Testament texts. It does not seem to be aware of the fact that "typology . . . makes many people uneasy and is perhaps the sign of a problem unresolved" and that "there is a Christian reading of the Old Testament which does not necessarily coincide with the Jewish reading."[15] *Notes* has pointed out the need for balancing "a number of pairs of ideas which express the relation between the two economies of the Old and New Testaments: Promise and Fulfillment, Continuity and Newness, Singularity and Universality, Uniqueness and Exemplary Nature."[16] It cannot be said that this balance is achieved in *Catechism*; in fact, supersessionist overtones can be heard in its christology and ecclesiology. To silence these voices *Catechism* would do well to incorporate into its exposition of the hermeneutics of the New Testament such paragraphs as the following:

It is essential to remember that the gospels represent theological reflections on the life and teaching of Jesus which, while historically based, were not intended by their authors to be eyewitness accounts. . . . Using methods familiar to us from contemporary Jewish apocalyptic and Essene writings (e.g., the Dead Sea Scrolls), as well as early rabbinic literature, the New Testament authors sought to

14. The following works on the relationship between the First and Second Testaments deserve notice: Clark M. Williamson, *Has God Rejected His People?* (Nashville: Abingdon Press, 1982); idem, *Interpreting Difficult Texts: Anti-Judaism and Christian Preaching* (Philadelphia: Trinity Press, 1989); *Biblical Studies: Meeting Ground of Jews and Christians*, ed. Helga Croner, Leon Klenicki and Lawrence Boadt (New York: Paulist Press, 1980); *God's Mercy Endures Forever: Guidelines on the Presentation of Jews and Judaism in Catholic Preaching* (Washington, D.C.: National Conference of Catholic Bishops, 1988).

15. *Notes*, 42.

16. *Notes*, 40. The document goes on to urge the catechist to show that "promise and fulfillment throw light on each other; newness lies in a metamorphosis of what was there before; the singularity of the people of the Old Testament is not exclusive and is open, in the divine vision, to a universal extension; the uniqueness of the Jewish people is meant to have the force of an example" (ibid).

explain their experience of Jesus in terms of their Jewish heritage, especially by using passages from the Hebrew Scriptures. When reading the prophets (e.g., Isaiah 7:14, 52–53; Hosea 11:1; Micah 5:1), the Evangelists interpreted Jewish hopes for the deliverance as foretelling Jesus' coming. *Such post-Resurrection insights do not replace the original intentions of the prophets.* Nor does Christian affirmation of the validity of the Evangelists' insight preclude the validity of post-NewTestament and present Jewish insight into the meaning of prophetic texts.[17]

2. *Catechism*'s christology, besides being markedly supersessionist, is also strangely muted on the Jewishness of Jesus, a point strongly emphasized by contemporary christology.[18] Because of its one-sided descending christology, it is unable to make it clear that:

Jesus was and always remained a Jew, his ministry was deliberately limited 'to the lost sheep of Israel' (Mt 15:24). Jesus is fully a man of his time, and of his environment— the Jewish Palestinian one of the first century, the anxieties and hopes of which he shared.[19]

17. *In Context*, 62. In introducing *Notes*, Bishop Jorge Mejia writes: "It is not always an easy matter to present the relations between both Testaments in a way that fully respects the validity of the Old Testament and shows its permanent usefulness for the Church.... In no way is 'typological' usage a devaluation of the validity proper to the Old Testament. Rather to the contrary.... The importance of the Old Testament for Judaism is underlined. So, too, is the importance of Jews and Christians hearing the Old Testament together, so that together, in the path opened by the prophetic tradition, we may become more deeply engaged as fellow partisans for humanity today.... It should be noted that the limits of 'typological' usage are acknowledged, and other possible ways of reading the Old Testament in relation to the New are not excluded" (p. 54). It is unfortunate that the limits of typology and the possibility of alternative interpretations are not explicitly acknowledged by *Catechism*.

18. On the Jewishness of Jesus, *Within Context* declares: "Jesus was born, lived and died a Jew of his times. He, his family and all his original disciples followed the laws, traditions and customs of his people. The key concepts of Jesus' teaching, therefore, cannot be understood apart from the Jewish heritage" (p. 59). The literature on Jesus and Judaism has grown by leaps and bounds; the following works are representative: E. P. Sanders, *Jesus and Judaism* (Philadelphia: Fortress, 1985); Gerard Sloyan, *Is Christ the End of the Law?* (Philadelphia: Westminster, 1978); Harvey Falk, *Jesus the Pharisee* (New York: Paulist Press, 1985); Bernard J. Lee, *The Galilean Jewishness of Jesus* (New York: Paulist Press, 1988); Leonard Swidler, *Yeshua: A Model for Moderns* (Kansas City: Sheed and Ward, 1988); James H. Charlesworth, *Jesus Within Judaism* (New York: Doubleday, 1988); and Michael Hilton and Gordian Marshall, *The Gospels and Rabbinic Judaism: A Study Guide* (New York: KTAV and ADL, 1988).

19. *Notes*, 44.

Catechism's description of Jesus' contemporaries leaves something to be desired as well. Its characterization of the Pharisees borders on caricature with its oblique reference to their "hypocritical casuistry" (no. 579).[20] True, *Catechism* does say that Jesus' relations with the Pharisees were not exclusively polemical, many of whom were his friends and many of whose teachings and practices were shared by Jesus (see no. 575). Nevertheless, it seems to take the gospels' account of the polemics between Jesus and the Pharisees at face value. There is no explicit acknowledgement that "some references hostile or less favorable to the Jews have their historical context in conflicts between the nascent Church and the Jewish community" and that "certain controversies reflect Christian Jewish relations long after the time of Jesus."[21] Though *Catechism* declines to judge the conscience of the participants in Jesus' trial, it comes perilously close to accusing the members of the Sanhedrin of bad faith when it affirms that they were acting out of not only ignorance but also the hardness of their unbelief (see no. 591). To accept Jesus' claim regarding his identity and mission, *Catechism* argues, requires "a mysterious death to self" (no. 591), a painful act the members of the Sanhedrin were allegedly unwilling to undergo.

3. In its account of Jesus' trial, *Catechism* rightly rejects the deicide charge and insists that "the church does not hesitate to impute to Christians the gravest responsibility for the torments inflicted upon Jesus" (no. 598).[22] Nevertheless, it seems to take the gospels' narratives of Jesus' passion as entirely eyewitness accounts of historical events and tends to gloss over the fact that the passion narratives are "post-Resurrection reflections from different perspectives on the meaning of Jesus' death and resurrection."[23] And even though *Catechism* warns that we should not impute collective responsibility on

---

20. For literature on the Pharisees, see Ellis Rivkin, *The Hidden Revolution: The Pharisees' Search for the Kingdom of God Within* (Nashville: Abingdon Press, 1978).

21. *Notes*, 46.

22. For studies on Jesus' trial, see Haim Cohen, *The Trial and Death of Jesus* (New York: KTAV, 1977); Donald Juel, *Messiah and Temple* (Missoula: Scholars Press, 1977); S.G.F. Brandon, *The Trial of Jesus of Nazareth* (New York: Stein and Day, 1979); Gerard Sloyan, *Jesus on Trial* (Philadelphia: Fortress, 1973); John T. Townsend, *A Liturgical Interpretation of Our Lord's Passion in Narrative Form* (New York: National Conference of Christians and Jews, 1985).

23. *Within Context*, 67.

the "Jews in Jerusalem as a whole" (no. 597) for Jesus' trial and death, unfortunately it continues to speak of "the Jewish authorities" in general in connection with Jesus' passion as if it were possible to identify with certainty who the "Jewish authorities" actually were. It has been remarked by biblical scholars, for instance, that the Pharisees are not depicted in the passion narratives as playing a significant role in Jesus' death. In general, had a paragraph such as the following been added in *Catechism*, a more accurate understanding of the passion story would have been facilitated:

Neither John nor Luke record a formal Sanhedrin "trial" of Jesus, making such a scene historically uncertain. Likewise there is a tendency from the earlier gospels (especially Mark) to the later (Matthew and John) to place more and more of the onus on "the Jews" and less on Pilate, who alone had the authority to order a crucifixion (Jn 18:31), a notion emphasized in Matthew's "hand-washing" scene (Mt 27:24). The use of the general term, "the Jews" in the Passion narrative of the Gospel of John can lead to a sense of collective guilt if not carefully explained.[24]

It is obvious that if *Catechism*'s uncritical retelling of the passion narratives is transmitted in catechesis and preaching without a careful attempt at contextualizing passages describing the conflicts between Jesus and various Jewish groups, it will lead to a misunderstanding of the nature of the gospels' account of Jesus' trial and death and even to anti-Jewish hostility, as history has shown all too well. In this context, the danger of anti-Semitism present in passion plays, still popular in many Catholic countries, should be duly noted.[25]

4. Finally, *Catechism*'s treatment of what it calls "the Old Law" (1962) is one-sidedly supersessionist and requires extensive amendment. Its repeated description of "the Old Law" as "the first stage of revealed Law" (nos. 1962 and 1980) and as "*a preparation for the Gospel*" (nos. 1964 and 1982) undermines the

24. *Within Context*, 68.
25. See Saul S. Friedman, *The Oberammergau Passion Play* (Carbondale: Southern Illinois University Press, 1984) and *Criteria for the Evaluation of Dramatization of the Passion* (Washington, DC: NCCB, 1988), a document issued by the Bishops' Committee for Ecumenical and Interreligious Affairs.

perennial validity of the Torah as God's will for the Jewish people, despite heroic protestations to the contrary. Above all, *Catechism's* sharp contrast between "the Old Law," "a law of bondage" which "shows what must be done but does not of itself give the strength, the grace of the Spirit, to fulfill it" (no. 1963) on the one hand and "the New Law or the Law of the Gospel" which is "the perfection here on earth of the divine law, natural and revealed . . . the interior law of charity" (no. 1965) and "the *grace of the Holy Spirit*" (no. 1966) on the other hand perpetuates the deleterious "Law vs. Gospel" motif of Reformation theology.

In contrast to this view, one must unambiguously speak of the Torah "as the revealed will of God, the response God expects of the people whom He has saved and with whom He has entered into an eternal, unbreakable covenant."[26] With regard to Paul's attitude to the Torah in particular, it must be remembered that "he never suggested that the Law (*Torah*) had ceased to be God's will for the Jewish people" and that regarding the Jews and the Torah, Paul states that "even after the founding of the Church, the relationship is enduring and valid, for 'God's gifts and call are irrevocable'."[27]

III. Going Beyond *Catechism* in Preaching and Instruction

Catechism has deliberately left the task of adaptation of doctrinal presentations and catechetical methods required by particular circumstances and needs to national and local catechisms and to those responsible for the teaching of the faith. In addition to those areas (e.g., covenant and election, the Scriptures, Torah and law, christology, and messiahship) in which its teachings, in my judgment, call for emendation and expansion, as suggested above, there are important

26. *Within Context*, 66. The text goes on to say: "Jesus accepted and observed the Law (cf. Gal. 4:4; Lk. 2:21–24), extolled respect for it, and invited obedience to it (Mt. 5:17–20). Therefore, it can never be valid to place Jesus' teaching (gospel) in fundamental opposition to the Torah. The dynamic reality that is Jewish Law should never be depicted as 'fossilized' or reduced to 'legalism'" (p. 66). *Guidelines* also states: "The Old Testament and the Jewish tradition founded upon it must not be set against the New Testament in such a way that the former seems to constitute a religion of only justice, fear and legalism, with no appeal to the love of God and neighbor (cf. Dt 6:5; Lv19:18; Mt 22:34–40)" (p. 34).
27. *Within Context*, 66.

themes in Jewish–Christian dialogue that *Catechism* has left unmentioned but must be brought to attention in catechesis and preaching in order to do full justice to the complex relationship between Judaism and Christianity. Limited space allows me to offer no more than hints on only the most important of these.

1. Catechesis and preaching must draw attention to the history of the Holocaust/Shoah and the deep-seated anti-Semitism in the Christian Church's theology and practice that was partially responsible for Hitler's attempted "final solution of the Jewish question."[28] Furthermore, preachers and catechists must be aware of the implications of the Shoah for the Christian discourse on God and Christ.[29]

2. Another explosive yet unavoidable issue in preaching and religious education is the question of the state of Israel. No doubt the foundation of the state of Israel is the single most important event in the Jewish history since the the the destruction of Jerusalem and the Second Temple by the Romans in 70 C.E. As Hans Küng points out, "the present-day state of Israel is a political entity, but by virtue of its whole tradition it also has a religious dimension."[30] Because of this religious dimension as well as of the church's responsibility for justice and peace catechesis and preaching cannot skirt the issue of the state of

28. The literature on the Holocaust is immense. From the Christian perspective, see David A. Rausch, *A Legacy of Hatred: Why Christians Must Not Forget the Holocaust* (Chicago: Moody, 1984). Michael McGarry has given a helpful account of the Holocaust in "The Holocaust: Tragedy of Christian History" in *Introduction to Jewish–Christian Relations*, ed. Michael Shermis and Arthur E. Zannoni (New York: Paulist Press, 1991), 63–86. Another very helpful presentation can be found also in Hans Küng, *Judaism: Between Yesterday and Tomorrow*, trans. John Bowden (New York: Crossroad, 1992), 219–81. For an evaluation of this monumental work, see my review in *Dialogue & Alliance* 6, no. 4 (1992–93): 144–47.

29. For a survey on God-talk after Auschwitz, see Hans Küng, *Judaism: Between Yesterday and Tomorrow*, trans. John Bowden (New York: Crossroad, 1992), 564–609; John T. Pawlikowski, *The Challenge of the Holocaust for Christian Theology* (New York: ADL, 1980); *The Holocaust as Interruption: A Question for Christian Theology*, ed. Elizabeth Schüssler Fiorenza and David Tracy (Edinburgh: T & T Clark, 1984); Clark M. Williamson, *A Guest in the House of Israel: Post-Holocaust Church Theology* (Louisville: Westminster/John Knox, 1993). For post-Holocaust christology, see Michael B. McGarry, *Christology after Auschwitz* (New York: Paulist Press, 1977) and John T. Pawlikowski, *Christ in the Light of the Christian Jewish Dialogue* (New York: Paulist Press, 1982); idem, *Jesus and the Theology of Israel* (Wilmington, DE: Michael Glazier, 1989); idem, "Christian Theological Concerns After Auschwitz," in *Visions of the Other: Jewish and Christian Theologians Assess the Dialogue*, ed. Eugene J. Fisher (New York: Paulist Press, 1994), 28–51.

30. *Judaism*, 522.

Israel and all its attendant political problems (e.g., the rights of the Palestinians).[31]

3. The foundation of the state of Israel as well as the continuing existence of Judaism as a world religion has shattered the supersessionist or displacement theology inherent in the Christian teaching of contempt against Jews and Judaism. It is necessary then that catechesis and preaching should approach Judaism not as "The Old Covenant" to which Christians claim to have succeeded as the "New Israel" or the "New People of God." Rather, if Judaism is to be understood at all, it must be studied as a *living* religion with which Christians have to enter into dialogue and from which they must learn in order to understand their *own* beliefs and practices. This task is incumbent upon catechists and preachers whether they expound Scripture or worship or morality or spirituality. Areas to be covered include biblical hermeneutics and Jewish religious traditions (e.g., doctrine of God, ethics, mission, prayer and liturgy, the relationship between Torah and gospel). In particular, catechetical preparation should explain how Christian sacraments, especially the eucharist, are rooted in the Jewish tradition and how the church's liturgical cycle of feasts parallels that of the synagogue, and draws its origins and continuing sustenance from it.[32]

31. For a helpful discussion of this issue, see Hans Küng, *Judaism*, 519–83 and Robert Andrew Everett, "The Land: Israel and the Middle East in Jewish–Christian Dialogue," in *An Introduction to Jewish–Christian Dialogue*, 87–117. For the theme of land in Jewish faith, see Walter Brueggemann, *The Land: Place as Gift. Promise. and Challenge in Biblical Faith* (Philadelphia: Fortress, 1977); W.D. Davies, *The Territorial Dimension of Judaism* (Berkeley: University of California, 1982); and Anthony Kenny, *Catholics, Jews and the State of Israel* (New York: Paulist Press, 1993).

32. On these issues, see *Within Context*, 62–72. Works that are useful in promoting an understanding of the connections between various aspects of Judaism and Christianity include: *Standing Before God: Studies on Prayer in Scripture and Tradition*, ed. Asher Finkel and Lawrence Frizzell (New York: KTAV, 1981); *The Lord's Prayer and Jewish Liturgy*, ed. J. Petuchowski and M. Brocke (New York: Seabury, 1978); *Spirituality and Prayer: Jewish and Christian Understandings*, ed. Leon Klenicki and Gabe Huck (New York: Paulist Press, 1983), Stuart E. Rosenberg, *Christians and Jews: The Eternal Bond* (New York: Frederick Ungar, 1985) and Gillian Feeley–Harnick, *The Lord's Table: Eucharist and Passover in Early Christianity* (Philadelphia: University of Pennsylvania Press, 1981). Very helpful works on how to present Jews and Christians in preaching are: Clark M. Williamson and Allen J. Allen, *Interpreting Difficult Texts: Anti-Judaism and Christian Preaching* (Philadelphia: Trinity International; London: SCM Press, 1989); Clark M. Williamson, *When Jews and Christians Meet* (St. Louis: CBP Press, 1989); *God's Mercy Endures Forever: Guidelines on the Presentation of Jews and Judaism in Catholic Preaching* (Washington, DC: National

4. Intimately connected with the issue of Judaism as a revealed living religion is the question of Christian mission to the Jews. Preaching and catechesis must squarely face the problem of whether Christians are called to carry out their mission to the Jews. *Catechism* deals with mission in detail (nos. 849–856), but does not have anything specific to say about mission to the Jews. It is universally agreed today that all forms of proselytism must be rejected in the pejorative sense of the term, i.e., the attempt to win converts by means of cajolery, pressure or intimidation, or other improper methods. But is it not possible to acknowledge further that Jews are already in a covenantal relationship with God and therefore that Christians are not called to convert Jews to their faith?[33] Rather, the mission of both Jews and Christians is to be understood as dialogue, mutual witness, and service to the world.[34]

It remains to be seen whether *Catechism*, like its predecessor, the *Roman Catechism*, will set the standard for future preaching and catechesis in the church. While its virtues are many, so are its inadequacies, especially in matters regarding the relationship between Judaism and Christianity. Its teachings on this theme can and must be corrected and complemented by recent developments in theology. More importantly, these church pronouncements and theological developments, if they are to bear fruit, must be incorporated into catechesis and worship. As Williamson eloquently puts it:

33. Christians who affirm the necessity of mission to the Jews often appeal to Matthew 28:19: "Make disciples of all the *ethné* (nations). "However, biblical scholars question this interpretation and suggest that *ethné* should be read in the Jewish context as referring to the *goyim* and therefore that the missionary mandate is not to be taken as applied to the Jews. See Daniel Harrington and Douglas Hare, "Make Disciples of All the Gentiles," *Catholic Biblical Quarterly* 37 (1975): 359–69.
34. On the church's mission to the Jews, there has been in the last decade a clear shift away from the missionary approach to the Jews toward a dialogical relationship between the church and the Jewish people. See *The Theology of the Churches and the Jewish People: Statements by the Council of Churches and its Member Churches*, edited with a commentary by Allan Brockway, Paul van Buren, Rolf Rendtorff, and Simon Schoon (Geneva: WCC Publications, 1988), pp. 173–76. See also *Issues in the Jewish–Christian Dialogue: Jewish Perspectives on Covenant. Mission and Witness*, ed. Helga Croner and Leon Klenicki (New York: Paulist Press, 1979); *Christian Mission – Jewish Mission*, ed. Martin Cohen and Helga Croner (New York: Paulist Press, 1982; *More Stepping Stones to Jewish–Christians Relation: An Unabridged Collection of Christian Documents 1975–1983*, compiled by Helga Croner (New York: Paulist Press, 1985).

Unless education, preaching, and worship in local congregations are appropriate to the good news of God's all-inclusive love and God's command that justice be done to all those whom God loves, none of the church's fine theological pronouncements on relations between Christian and Jews will, in the end, be worth a fig.[35]

---

35. *A Guest in the House of Israel*, 47.

INTRODUCTION TO SECTION TWO

Howard Clark Kee

It is an important task to understand the historical and exegetical principles which are involved in recognizing the origins of anti-Judaism in the preaching traditions of the Christian churches, and in seeking to remove them. This need has been addressed in section one of this volume. But it is equally important and demanding that examples be made available for readers—both lay and clergy—of sermons in which these issues are dealt with effectively.

The second part of this volume consists of sermons which are admirable demonstrations of ways in which the historic tensions and hostilities between Jews and Christians can be overcome. Those who have contributed these sermons come from diverse backgrounds: churches and academic institutions, Catholic and Protestant. Following the sermons that are here reproduced is a perceptive analytical essay which highlights the contributions of each sermon and articulates the issues and methods by which Jewish–Christian tensions and misunderstandings have been addressed in exemplary fashion. It is hoped that, together with the issues identified in section one, these sermons will serve as models to help achieve the aim of this volume: removing Anti-Judaism from the pulpit.

CHAPTER ONE

Deadly Memories: Confronting Anti-Jewish Elements in Scripture

Carol Ann Morrow

However festive and tinged with Resurrection light it may be, the celebration of Easter has its underside. Holy Week's history includes episodes of insult and violence toward Jews. Synagogues have been destroyed and innocent Jews murdered by Catholics acting on the ugly falsehood that Jews required the blood of a young Christian to prepare the Passover meal. "Christ-killers" is a chilling epithet still heard today.

The Solemn Prayers of Good Friday in the Catholic liturgy have long included a prayer for the Jewish people. While that prayer once called them "faithless," the text now reads, "Let us pray for the Jewish people, the first to hear the Word of God."

Many church leaders and theologians, following Pope John Paul II's lead, have urged a thorough rethinking of the Catholic Church's relationship to Judaism. "It is no secret that many of our past [theological] formulations have seriously distorted the role of the Jewish people in human salvation," Chicago Cardinal Joseph L. Bernardin has said. "These distortions undoubtedly played a role in the persecutions borne by Jewish communities in so many parts of the world and tragically helped provide a seedbed for Christian collaboration with the fundamentally anti-religious philosophy of Nazism."

Certain passages within the New Testament itself are responsible for skewing the Christian view of Judaism. Cardinal Johannes Willebrands led the drafting of a 1985 Vatican document which states: "It cannot be ruled out that some references hostile or less than favorable to the Jews have their historical context in conflicts between the nascent Church and the Jewish community. Certain controversies reflect Christian–Jewish relations long after the time of Jesus. To establish this is of capital importance if we wish to bring out the meaning of certain Gospel texts for the Christians of today."

Father John Pawlikowski, internationally known for his work in Jewish–Catholic relations, has made clear that the Gospel texts themselves can cause problems and has written notes for homilists urging them to express respect for the Judaism of Jesus' day. He warns that, unless the preaching of Holy Week expresses the love Jesus had for the Torah and for his Jewish inheritance, "our yearly commemoration of it will retain the potential for anti-Semitism."

Two scholars who help Christians wrestle with troubling Scripture passages are Sister Ruth Graf, R.S.M., and Arthur Dewey, theology professors at Xavier University, Cincinnati, Ohio. The two have run study weeks designed for Christians willing to grapple with the challenges of scriptural interpretation. Their approach could prove helpful for preachers seeking to design sermons related to significant biblical texts.

Using as background reading the work of Catholic historian Edward Flannery, former adviser to the U.S. bishops on Catholic Jewish relations, Sister Ruth and Dr. Dewey cite original texts of early Church Fathers as well as *Nostra Aetate* and other Vatican texts. "Nobody is teaching a prejudice against Jews," says Sister Ruth, yet she finds that many of those she's taught start out extremely anti-Jewish, saying outright that "Jews *should* suffer because they killed Christ," using Scripture to support their claim. "Unless this issue is addressed, the possibility of yet another Holocaust is very real indeed."

Arthur Dewey emphasizes that "We must rearrange our imaginative world view, our emotional furniture, as it were." To do this he and Sister Ruth run weeklong workshops during which they concentrate specifically on various passages from Scripture.

"What Will the Owner of the Vineyard Do?"

The first passage they tackle is the story of the Tenant Farmers as recorded in Mk 12:1–12 and later in Mt 21:33–46. The parable is one of a series of polemical addresses.

A landowner rents his vineyard, then sends his servants numerous times to collect what is owed him. They are mistreated, so as a last resort he sends his son. The tenants kill him. *"What do you suppose the owner of the vineyard will do? He will come and destroy those tenants, and turn his vineyard over to others"* (Mk 12:8).

The two teachers lead study groups through a personal wrestling with these passages. They encourage class members to rethink the text, to shake the American fixation with verbatim understanding, and to enter into the history of the text and the polemical style so typical of both Old and New Testaments and of the historical period as a whole.

Dewey provides a colorful explanation of Judaism in the ancient world. "The use of stereotype was integral to the worldview of the time." The hero must be victorious. This rhetorical hyperbole, he suggests, is not unlike "the commentary on the Super Bowl or the World Series." Clichés, easily remembered formulas, and use of types were crucial to telling a story.

Encouraging comparison of texts, the professor urges students to search out common elements, consider the context, look up references to the Old Testament, and determine to whom any pronoun might refer. Participants are taxed by the effort of shaking off "easy" interpretations that the "chief priests, the scribes and the elders" mentioned in Mark 11:27 had to be the villains of the piece. Eventually they raise questions that are new to them:

— Is the vineyard of Mark the same vineyard as described in Isaiah 5?

— What does the word *son* mean here? Kings were called "sons of God." Prophets were "sons."

— Could "he will give the vineyard to others" simply mean to Jews other than the ones he was addressing in this parable?

— The passage says that the "they" of this parable wanted to arrest Jesus. Did the Jews have the power to arrest anyone?

— Wouldn't a Jewish listener interpret this to mean, "If the leaders mess up, something bad will happen"? They would see it as part of the ongoing ups and downs of their relationship with God, not as a "final solution," wouldn't they?

— And, finally, is this critique directed to just one group, and not to the whole Jewish people?

Dewey and Sister Ruth are quick to affirm the last question.

They comment: "To think of this passage as referring to the whole Jewish people is *deadly*. To see that the Gospels are complex and require thoughtful interpretation frees us to respond creatively to the questions: What did it mean then? What can it mean now?"

"Let His Blood Be on Us"

"Many, I know, respect the Jews and think that their present way of life is a venerable one. This is why I hasten to uproot and tear out this deadly opinion." These words are taken from a sermon by St. John Chrysostom (circa 344–407). Historian Edward Flannery sees the fourth century, the time of Chrysostom, as critical. Flannery defends Christian polemics and actions against Jews up to that period as being provoked by challenges from the Jewish nation which was stronger than the newly converted Christian minority. Also, he observes, critiques were largely on a theological or apologetical plane and did not incite to violence. Christian pastors could see that their converts (nearly all Jews) were not well instructed in their new faith and wandered back and forth between Judaism and belief in Jesus.

Chrysostom, the golden-tongued young preacher of Antioch, is characterized by Flannery as guilty of a "grave lapse from charity and common justice." Sister Ruth reads extensive excerpts from Chrysostom's *First Discourse*: "But I must get back to those who are sick [Judaizers, or Christians who are friendly with Jews]. Consider, then, with whom they are sharing their fasts. It is with those who shouted: 'Crucify him. Crucify him,' with those who said, 'His blood be upon us and upon our children'. . . . What else do you wish me to tell you? Shall I tell you of their plundering, their covetousness, their abandonment of the poor, their thefts, their cheating in trade?"

It was the average convert's love for Judaism and things Jewish that inspired such diatribe, Flannery adds. Chrysostom was worried that his flock might return to Judaism and abandon their newfound Christian faith. Instead, the fourth century was an hour of triumph for the church. Emperor Constantine's deathbed conversion led to the passage of laws which translated theological attitudes into legal constraints.

As Sister Ruth unfolds this early church history, the power of Scripture and of sermons citing it gain new respect from the workshop group. It is an easy transition to the text of the Passion as narrated in Matthew 27.

Two basic facts loom large in trying to interpret Matthew's Passion account. Jesus was a Jew. The Jews have been condemned by the prophets more times than the average bible reader can count. That condemnation or "prophetic critique," Dewey explains, was to elicit their conversion, their "return to the Lord." It was a warning, not a final eviction notice.

Matthew 27 includes the trial before Pilate as well as the crucifixion, death, and burial of Jesus. It contains the passage cited against the Jews by Chrysostom. *"The whole people said in reply, 'Let his blood be on us and on our children'"* (Matt. 27:25).

As groups read this passage, Sister Ruth recalls, they become newly conscious of anti-Judaic elements in Scripture. She recalls one woman who was "horrified by the Passion narrative, but just as horrified that nobody did anything by way of correction. When people hear the story, especially in the drama of Holy Week, it gets embedded in their minds." But what else can be made of it besides what seems so obvious, that the Jews asked for any trouble that might come their way from then on?

Plenty, interjects Dewey. First of all, he points out, Jesus was killed by Romans. The question of Jewish involvement in the death of Christ is debatable. The Gospel texts are not historical but polemical, meant to prove a point. The trial scene is completely unorthodox, that is, not according to the way it would have been done if it had been guided by Jewish influence.

According to Fr. Pawlikowski, "Jesus was killed by *some* Jews and *some* Romans, but Christians have played up Jewish involvement. . . . Historically, Romans probably had more to do with the death of Jesus than the Christian Scriptures lead one to think." Available historical records indicate that Pilate was a cruel tyrant, but it was unwise to criticize publicly the rule of Rome at the time the Gospels were being recorded.

"And just where were the disciples during this trial?" asks Dewey with a smile, knowing that most participants would recall that the disciples fled the scene. This admission prompts his next question, "So how did *they* know what happened? If they all fled, they are *not* good witnesses!"

This observation, while made with humor, strikes a chord in the group. People don't like to hear that what they are so familiar with might not be exactly true, or not true in the way they had thought. Dewey reminds his listeners that the Scriptures are not harmonious and encourages them to live with that disharmony. He invites them to read all four narratives and to discover discrepancies and look for patterns; try to determine the concerns of each Gospel writer; and compare them with Wisdom 2:12–20 and Isaiah's references to the Suffering Servant. "Then you need to consider what question the passage is meant to answer. In this instance, I'd say it's, "What is the meaning of the death of Jesus?' Based on the evidence, my assessment is that it's a polemic showing that people screwed up and killed the righteous one.

"You need to see what Matthew has added, remembering that he was writing for the Jewish people. He needs to show that the Jewish leadership was corrupt, to contrast the Jesus Jews with the Pharisaic Jews." Dewey points out that the crowd chose Barabbas, who was probably a type conveniently named Bar/Abba, or "Son of the Father." The writer's intent, he says, is to point a finger. "You chose the *wrong* son of the Father, people."

"Our Father Is Abraham"

Using Flannery as a source, Sister Ruth then reads a litany of increasing historical oppression leading up to a discussion of John 8: 39–45, the evangelist's strongest indictment against the Jewish people. To grapple with this passage requires some sense of the history of the Johannine community, a group coalescing in the mid-fifties after the death of Jesus. John's followers were probably persecuted by the Jews, which bound them closer to one another, and cemented their opposition to the "sons of the devil," as they began to characterize the Jews. By the year 90 they saw themselves as "Sons of the Father" while the Jews became the "seeing blind" of John 9.

Workshop participants are led to see how these historical events and Gospel passages helped shape later Christian characterization of Jews as anonymous, faceless persons, resulting in dire consequences by fostering anti-Semitism.

The workshop in scriptural study concludes with discussions on Paul and on the relationship between Jesus and the

Pharisees as presented in Matthew. When each author is read in context, it becomes clear that they come out of a Jewish milieu and are working through specific problems facing their communities. For instance, Dewey suggests that scholarly opinion is shifting toward a more "Jewish" Paul, a Paul who was proud of his own Jewishness, who responded pragmatically to problem situations but who continued to observe the Torah himself.

The aim of the workshops is to help Christians bring to the surface and exorcise "deadly memories" within Christianity about Jews and Judaism. Their methods and message deserve the attention of all preachers seeking to shed the light of truth on Scripture texts both Jews and Christians treasure.

CHAPTER TWO

The Root That Supports Us

Wallace M. Alston, Jr.

> *If you do boast, remember it is not you that*
> *support the root, but the root that supports you.*
> Romans 11:18

The delightful movie, *Driving Miss Daisy,* set and filmed in
the Druid Hills neighborhood of Atlanta, where I once lived
and went to school, reminded me of something that I dare not
forget; namely, that one of the first acts of public violence in
that city after the Supreme Court decision to desegregate the
schools was the bombing of a prominent Jewish synagogue. I
remember thinking at the time how strange it was that, for
fear of the Blacks, the Jews had been attacked. Now I know it
was not so strange at all—demented, perhaps, but rather typical. The same thing can be documented in every part of our
country, and in all parts of the globe, and in nearly every period of history. Social and political frustration, time and time
again, has been expressed in the visitation of violence upon
the Jews.

This morning I want to bring into the open the issue of anti-
Semitism, and I want to do so not as a disinterested observer,
but as a Christian. The issue of anti-Semitism was not laid to
rest with the defeat of Adolf Hitler. It is still with us and may
even be on the rise in our time and in our town. Christians, of
all people, must be on their guard against this enemy of the
Christian faith. We must be prepared to stand up and be
counted whenever it raises its ugly head—in home or school;
at a cocktail party, in a joke, or at work. We do well to remember that Jesus was not a white, Anglo-Saxon Protestant who
was much like us but a dark skinned Semite who was never a
Christian but always a Jew, who honored his Judaism, who
kept its traditions, and who had no thought of giving it up by

converting to another religion. Anti-Semitism of any kind is an act of violence against Jesus and against his people and an out-right denial of everything he stood for, said, and was.

One indication that the issue of anti-Semitism is still with us is the manner in which the Christian season of Lent, and espe-cially Holy Week, annually causes many Jews and their loved ones to shudder. We must be careful about the overtones and undertones of the things read and said about the death of Jesus from the pulpit, especially at a time when anti-Semitism appears to be gaining a degree of respectability again.

Another indication that the issue of anti-Semitism is still with us was a recent Easter Sunday editorial in the *New York Times* which reminded readers that "the roots of Judaism and Christianity are deeply intertwined," that "their separation during the first century A.D. occurred with bitterness," and that the imprint of this bitterness is still to be found in the sacred Scriptures of the Christian Church. There is no doubt about that. There is anti-Semitism in the New Testament. The Gospel of John is probably the most anti-Semitic book in the New Testament. It comes to us out of an intense struggle within first century Judaism between Jews who saw in Jesus the presence of the Messiah and Jews who did not. The Gospel of John reflects that struggle within Judaism and the pain of those Jews who were expelled from the synagogue. Though this specific incident is now a matter of the distant past, the animus of those quarrels continues to stir enmity in the human community, the article suggested, "from the blood libels of the Middle Ages, to the Nazi Holocaust, to the bizarre reemergence under glasnost of anti-Semitism in the Soviet Union."

A few weeks ago, I watched the reenactment of the death of Jesus in a lovely Bavarian village located, ironically enough, only a few short miles from the site of Hitler's mountaintop retreat —wondering what some people in the audience must be thinking as they watched Germans trying to act like Jews for a change, hearing "auf Deutsch" those words that have under-girded a wretched history of violence with an easy conscience: "His blood be upon us and on our children" (Matt. 27:25), remembering that it all happened in my lifetime and recogniz-ing that it could probably happen again.

So, how is it today between Christians and Jews? Where are we as Christian people today in our attitudes and actions with respect to the Jewish community? The Anti-Defamation League recorded nearly two thousand anti-Semitic incidents in 1994. Are they oversensitive and unnecessarily defensive? Or is there still a cancer in our individual and corporate soul for which we have yet to find a cure? Three points call for emphasis and clarification:

1. *First, as Christians, I hope we are at a place where we can freely and gratefully admit how much the Jewish presence means to our existence as Christian people.* This may sound a bit selfish, and it may not be the most important thing we have to say, but it is a place to begin, if only because we have not always accepted it as so.

Christians stand in a different relation to Judaism than to any other religion in the world. Judaism is the religion above all others that provides us with a sacred history long predating the presence in time of Jesus of Nazareth. Our differences are real and important; but they are differences between members of the same family whose traditions have their own distinctive features, but whose God is one, the God of the patriarchs and prophets.

The Hebrew Scriptures, of course, was the first Christian Bible, the primary authority for the faith of the early church and for its understanding of itself and its Lord. In the second-century A.D., a powerful, wealthy man named Marcion — son of a bishop and a fine Christian in his own right — came to Rome, joined the church, gave liberally of his wealth for its life and work, and began to teach. Marcion was overwhelmed by God's grace whereby God forgives our sin, and he could not reconcile this God with the God of the Hebrew Scriptures, whom Marcion felt to be full of wrath and anger. So Marcion tried to get rid of the Hebrew Scriptures altogether, being convinced that the church was making a mistake in aligning itself with the religion and literature of the Jews.

But in 144 A.D., the church said "No" to Marcion, reclaiming what came to be known in the Christian community as the Old Testament. Those first Christians knew that grace was not the only thing that one must say about God, that soteriology (how one may be saved) was not the sole concern of theology, and that grace must always be seen in the light of God's truth and God's justice.

They resisted the temptation to spiritualize the gospel by lifting it out of, and holding it above, the realms of nature and history. It is the Hebrew Scriptures, at times more than the New, that has sustained people in times of personal or political anguish.

"My thoughts and feelings seem to be getting more and more like the Hebrew Scriptures," wrote Dietrich Bonhoeffer from his prison cell in 1943; "and no wonder, I have been reading it much more than the New for the last few months. It is only when one knows the ineffability of the name of God that one can utter the name of Jesus Christ. It is only when one loves life and the earth so much that without them everything would be gone, that one can believe in the resurrection and a new world. It is only when one submits to the law that one can speak of grace, and only when one sees the anger and wrath of God hanging like grim realities over the head of one's enemies that one can know something of what it means to love and forgive them. I don't think it is Christian to want to get to the New Testament too soon and too directly . . . . You cannot and must not speak the last word before you have spoken the next to last. We live on the next to last word, and believe on the last, don't we?"

Not long before Marcion came to Rome, one Paul of Tarsus reminded Christian people there that they owed their very existence to their brothers and sisters of the synagogue. If you are of a mind to boast, Paul said,

> . . . *remember it is not you that support the root,*
> *but the root that supports you.*

2. *Second I think we are at a place in the relationship between Christian and Jew where Christian people simply must understand and accept the fact that, although we may want to draw closer to our Jewish brothers and sisters, it may still be very hard, if not impossible, for many Jewish people to respond in kind.* The long years of pain and oppression, inflicted by self-proclaimed "Christian" cultures on Jews, will not be soon or easily overcome.

Some Jews genuinely desire better relations with Christians, if only Christians will leave their theological baggage at home when they come to call. "Must we love each other?" asked Rabbi Richard Rubenstein in a Catholic journal. "As a Jew I feel an acute sense of discomfort when I read that Catholics must love Jews—this is an imperative. . . . There is really too much that separates us. There ought to be a realistic alternative to the either–or of love and hate. Why can't we rest content with learning to appreciate and understand each other? . . . The real tragedy of the Judeo–Christian encounter is that it is almost impossible for Christians to see Jews simply as men rather than as actors in the divine drama involving the eternal salvation of mankind. . . . It would be far better were Christians and Jews to regard each other simply as persons."

Others of the Jewish community want no dealings with Christians at all. "What was started at the Council of Nicaea," said Rabbi Eliezer Berkovits, "was duly completed in the concentration camps and crematoria." At this stage, he said, it would be as immoral as it would be emotionally impossible for a sensitive, historically conscious Jew to have anything to do with Christians at all. "All we want of Christians is that they keep their hands off us and our children."

Those words are hard to hear and hard to bear, but hear and bear them we must, I think, for some time to come. The judgment of their continued existence upon a history that seems determined to do them in may be our sign of the historical reality of God's incredibly steadfast love, and of the staying power of the covenant, and thus of the validity of our ultimate hope. The persistent presence, the continued witness, of the Jewish community in the midst of a world that has tried to prevent its survival may be our best evidence that God is, and that God is serious about the promise to Abraham, and thus that God may be trusted to be serious about the promise made to us. So, once again, if you are tempted to boast,

> . . . *remember it is not you that support the root,*
> *but the root that supports you.*

3. Third, I think we are at a place where we simply must stop trying and disassociate ourselves from all fundamentalist and evangelical efforts that continue to try to convert Jews to Christianity. It may surprise you to hear a Christian minister say this, but I think we Christians must stop trying to convert Jews to Christianity. They are not objects for our "thirst for souls!" "I had rather enter Auschwitz," said Rabbi Abraham Heschel, "than be an object of conversion."

Christians do believe without apology that Jesus of Nazareth is the long-awaited Messiah of Israel; that he lived, died, and rose from the dead for all people; and that to embrace him is life's greatest joy. But conversion is not the way to share that joy with the Jews. First, because it turns the much needed dialogue, wherein old misunderstandings, prejudices, and stereotypes might be overcome, into a power-game of who is going to win out over the other in the end—and that is far from any decent sense of Christian evangelism.

Second, because of the historical, psychological, and sociological scars left by Christian enthusiasm on the Jewish memory. To many Jews, Christianity is a symbol of oppression, persecution, torture, and death. "The two faiths despite differences are sufficiently alike for the Jew to find God more easily in terms of his own religious heritage," said Reinhold Niebuhr, "than by subjecting himself to the hazards of guilt feeling involved in a conversion to a faith, which whatever its excellences, must appear to him as a symbol of an oppressive majority culture." Perhaps the best witness a Christian could make to the Jew is to encourage and help him or her to be a more faithful Jew.

Third, there are theological reasons that militate against conversion, having to do with the role and place of both synagogue and church in the greater economy of God. Paul Tillich made the point, for example, that the mission of the Jews until the end of history will be to bear witness against idolatry. The Jews represent God's prophetic word spoken against all institutions, including the church, that create for themselves gods in human or institutional form. Franz Rosenzweig, a Jewish thinker, called Christianity the missionary arm of Israel, the outreach of the God of Abraham, Isaac, and Jacob to the gentile world. He suggested that the gentile world would come to faith in this God only through the agency of Christianity.

Will Herberg, another Jewish scholar, also saw Christianity as Judaism's apostle. "Christianity arose," he wrote, "at a great crisis in Israel's history, as an outgoing movement to bring the God of Israel to the gentiles by bringing the gentiles into the covenant." By means of Judaism, men and women become members of the covenant by birth. By means of Christianity, men and women become members of the covenant by adoption. Why is it not possible to believe that the tasks of Jews and Christians in the world are complementary rather than contradictory, and make our relationships one with the other reflections of that belief?

When the late Pope John XXIII received a delegation of Jewish visitors early in his pontificate, he walked over to them with open arms and said: "I am Joseph, your brother" (Ex 45:4). That is where we need to be, it seems to me, if it is not where we are today in the relationship between Christians and Jews. Perhaps God will find some new way to use these two members of God's one covenant family to serve the human good and to bring glory to God's great name.

It would be unseemly for Christians to boast about anything we have done to bring this new day of mutuality, justice, and peace to pass. But,

> *If you do boast, remember it is not you that support the*
> *root, but the root that supports you.*

Thanks be to God. Amen.

CHAPTER THREE

Schindler's List — Our Lists

Nancy M. Malone

(Is. 42.1–4; Ps. 22. 1–8, 22–26; Jn. 1.29–34)

First, some facts:

1) The Holocaust did happen. Despite the profound regret of most Germans, of most Christians, and of people of good will throughout the world—and despite the denial that it happened—it did. If you have any doubt of it, and even if you haven't, please see—if you haven't already—Claude Lanzmann's *Shoah*, an eight-hour documentary of interviews with people, survivors among them, who were eyewitnesses or participants in some way in it. Or visit the Holocaust Museum in Washington, D.C.

2) Jesus was a Jew. A faithful, practicing Jew. Let that fact sink in.

3) There are in the Christian Scriptures anti-Semitic—or more accurately, anti-Judaic passages—or passages that easily lend themselves to anti-Semitic interpretation. The reasons for their appearance are complex but explainable, not praiseworthy, not unregrettable, but explainable.

4) Christians throughout the centuries have been the chief perpetrators of crimes against the Jews.

5) The Holocaust raises profound theological questions for Jews about which we have no right to speak. The Holocaust raises profound theological questions for Christians about which we must speak.

Let us begin today with the theological questions raised by the Christian symbol of the cross. A recent issue of *Cross Currents* (Spring, 1995) carries an excellent article by Mary Boys entitled: "The Cross: Should a Symbol Betrayed Be Reclaimed?" In the article, Boys, a Roman Catholic nun, briefly traces the omnipresence and depth of meaning of this symbol in her life as a Christian (more present, more deeply for Catholics, perhaps, because of the sacramental nature of Catholicism). And she describes her coming to awareness "of a compelling and tragic story of two people [Christians and Jews] who carry radically different memories of a single symbol." From the time that Jesus died on the cross, a form of execution that was "brutal and bloody, yet cheap and effective," leading Paul to speak of the crucified one "emptying himself, taking the form of a slave, humbling himself in obedience unto death, even death on a cross" (Phil 2:7–8), it was not long— before the completion of the Christian Scriptures, in fact—that this symbol was being used in a polemical way against the synagogue to accuse the Jews of crucifying Jesus. Late in the second century, as the Christology of the divine nature of Christ developed, the charge became one of deicide, the murder of God; and by the time of Constantine's famous vision of the cross with the message "*Conquer* by this," the symbol had clearly been transformed from one of suffering and humiliation to one of domination. In the Crusades, so called because of the cross emblazoned on the tunic of each crusader, the cross became a clarion call to liberate the Holy Land from the infidels. But there were "infidels" closer to home, the Jews, who suffered persecution and death from renegade crusading armies. And so on, to our own times, to Auschwitz, the Auschwitz of the death camp and of the controversy over the Carmelite convent there with a cross implanted in front of it. I am in no way doing justice to the rich detail and coherence of Boys' article, but the argument is clear—of the same symbol carrying radically different meanings for two different peoples. Read it please.

Boys does not mention—and I remember my horror on discovering it—that the swastika is a form of the cross: "a symbol or ornament in the form of Greek cross with the ends of the arms extended at right angles all in the same rotary direction," as the dictionary says. Which brings us to our subject, the

Holocaust, Shoah, as the Jews prefer to call it. I'm afraid that the whole story is there in that sick, twisted symbol, and the evil uses to which it was put. Many of you no doubt have seen *Schindler's List*; I would urge those of you who haven't to do so. Each of us will carry from the film something different, some lasting impressions. These were mine: weeping compassion for the poor hapless Jews, poor hapless human beings, herded— herded from their lovely homes into the ghetto; from the ghetto to the cattle cars; from the cars to the camps, through the showers—of water or gas—some to the ovens. And the correlative of that herding, in every instance, of functionaries, setting up their little tables, with their lists, to catalog the people, to catalog the booty, the loot from the plundering of their homes, to catalog personal possessions—shoes, rings, bracelets, eye-glasses. Schindler's was not the only list. Among the many other things that it was, the Shoah was an immense bureaucratic enterprise, lots of lists, made by lots of little people. And over against those images of crowds, herds, functionaries, and their lists, the image of the little girl in the red coat, hurrying alone, with all the purposefulness of a six-year-old hurrying to school, to get herself to safety. We see the red coat, the only color in a handsomely stark black and white film, later. These impressions led me to reflect on power, on powerlessness, and on our share, as Christians, in both, especially in regard to the Jewish people.

Most of us, fortunately and unfortunately, do not have the power or the opportunity to do either great good or great evil. The evil of a Hitler is beyond us, almost incomprehensible to us. But we do have the power, or the weakness, that leads us to do the little evils that cooperate with great evil: the fear of disapproval from authority or even peers; fear of the possible loss of a job or a privilege; unthinking capitulation to a dominant ethos—sexism, racism,. ethnicism, anti-Semitism; greed and envy toward those who have more or are more than we are— smarter, more successful; control of information or people in our own little domains. These, and a misshapen belief about Jews as Christ-killers, used as an excuse, perhaps, probably moved most people to cooperate in the great evil that was the Holocaust. Little people making their little lists. We all have them, our little lists. Where in all of this does our power lie and where our powerlessness?

Let us go back to Jesus, the Jew, as portrayed in the Gospel narrative: born away from home (Galilee, a place of no economic or cultural distinction) as a result of a bureaucratic decision by the occupying Roman power that a census be taken. Forced to flee to Egypt, as a perceived threat to the Roman tetrarch Herod, the infant Jesus became a refugee. He was imprisoned, tortured, executed as a criminal by the Romans for the same reason. Named the Lamb of God and presented in the language of the Suffering Servant from the prophet Isaiah, the only signs of worldly power bestowed on him were made in ridicule and irony: the crown of thorns, the scepter, the inscription on the cross, "Jesus of Nazareth, king of the Jews." He healed a leper, a blind man, a woman with a hemorrhage. He ate with a tax collector, welcomed a prostitute. He told the poor and the despised that the reign of God was for them. He challenged human religious laws that claimed to bestow righteousness by their observance, instead of as the free gift of God that it is. Where was the threat to power in this? Where was/is Jesus' power?

Jesus' power lay in his authority, his *exousia*, as the Greek has it. "He spoke with great authority," the people said. His authority lay in knowing who he was—the dearly beloved child of God, "my chosen one in whom I delight" in the language of Isaiah. And this, the truth, made him free—free from fear, from the threats of misused power, free from sin, free to love, free to die on a cross. Of ourselves we are not free, from fear or to love as we are commanded to love. We don't know who we are; we don't know who God is. We are sinners, even against our will.

But he told us over and over again, "Do not fear." "I have overcome the world," he said. He is the Lamb of God who takes away the sins of the world. What an astonishing statement! What could it possibly mean? I no longer believe that it means, as in some kind of divine financial transaction, that his death paid our debt to God and we're home free. No, for me it can only mean that as the Risen One, living now, he takes away our sins now, frees us from our fears, pours forth his own Spirit into our hearts, and empowers us to love and to live as he did. If we let him. If we want him to. If we let go of our false selves and find our true selves in God. If we give up our pathetic efforts to be powerful in our own right. If we pick up our cross and follow him.

And what cross is that, besides the cross of our own poor false selves and the cross of suffering that marks every human life? It is the cross that is the symbol not of domination, as it was for Constantine and is now for the Klan, as the swastika was for the Nazis, and is now for the neo-Nazis, but of *resistance to oppression*, in whatever form. It was not long ago, before World War II, that there were quotas for Jews in universities like Cornell. There are not now, at least official ones, but there are still disturbing stories of swastikas being painted on the doors of Jewish students here and there. There are clubs, college clubs and country clubs, that by policy or unwritten agreement do not admit Jews. Do you belong to them? There are the oppressive experiences of stereotyping, of anti-Semitic remarks and jokes. Pick up the cross of resistance; reclaim the symbol of *Jesus'* cross. Resist.

It is also the cross with the moral imperative to repent, deeply repent, of the evil visited upon Jews in its name. And within that imperative, it seems to me, comes an obligation to learn about, to study, to be informed about the Holocaust, so that, at the very least, its reality cannot be denied. And it is the cross as the discipline of treating every human being as an individual person, not as a member of a race, or class, or sexual orientation, or whatever. Not as one of the crowd—the herd —but as unique, as unique as the little girl in the red coat, a dearly loved child of God.

Such small things require in a way so little of us. No more than was required, in a way, of the functionaries. May it be given to us, as it was to Schindler—who was, after all, no saint —to have our little lists recorded in the book of life and not of death. "Lamb of God, you take away the sins of the world." Take away the sins of our selfish, fearful, sometimes mean little hearts. In the name of our Creator, Redeemer, Sanctifier. In the name of the Father, and the Son, and the Holy Spirit. Amen.

This was a sermon delivered in Sage Chapel, Cornell University, commemorating the Holocaust, Yom Hashoah.

CHAPTER FOUR

Resurrection, the Holocaust, and Forgiveness: A Sermon for Eastertime

Stanley Hauerwas

Job 42:1–6
Acts 5:12a, 17–22, 25–29
John 20:19–31

So what do we do now? We have had our resurrection, our Easter. It was a grand time—the high point of the church year liturgically, spiritually, and aesthetically. But what do we do now? Many of us feel emotionally drained and are not sure we want to go on to the next step. Indeed we are not even sure we know what the next step should be. Resurrection after all is a hard act to follow, for nothing seems capable of topping that one. Its dramatic nature seems to wash out anything that might follow.

We should not, therefore, feel surprised that we experience something of an emotional letdown after Easter. But I suspect that our letdown has more profound roots than simply coming down from a liturgical and emotional high. For resurrection, in spite of all the significant theological claims we make about it and what many of us may well think we believe about its significance, seems more like a retreat than a victory. We claim that through the resurrection God has done marvelous things for us, but in fact we feel like God has left us holding the bag with little resources to know how to go on. Resurrection, rather than being the supreme claim that God remains with us, in our day seems to symbolize that just when the going gets tough—that is, just when we have to face the fact that we have to go on living day by day—God takes a flyer. Resurrection may not be good news, but bad news about the God that could not take it. God has escaped from our lives leaving us with sentimental advice that it would certainly be a good thing if we loved one another.

Resurrection as the felt absence of God from our lives seems particularly powerful when we must face, as we must this Sunday, the Holocaust. All those who celebrate the absence of God as providing the space and arena for human freedom have been run aground on this reality. We live in a world where six million Jews and ten million other noncombatants were put to death by people not too unlike you and me. How are we to "explain" that one, for like evil itself, every explanation seems to trivialize the reality. Who can blame God for exiting from this kind of world? I do not particularly want to be involved with it either.

But I am involved with it. I am the inheritor of the history and benefits of a civilization that brutally and cold-bloodedly put six million people to death for no other reason than they were acknowledged as God's chosen people. And like Job we cry out for an explanation—how and why could this happen to your own and why and how could it be perpetrated in a culture formed by those who claim to worship the same God as the Jews? And like Job all we feel we get back is claims of power and incomprehensibility made all the more unsatisfactory by being packaged in magnificent poetry:

> *Behold, Behemoth,*
> > *which I made as I made you;*
> *he eats grass like an ox.*
> > *Behold, his strength in his loins,*
> *and his power in the muscles of his belly.*
> > *He makes his tail stiff like a cedar;*
> *the sinews of his thighs are knit together.*
> > *His bones are tubes of bronze,*
> *his limbs like bars of iron.* (Job 40:15–18)

And so it goes—on to the Leviathan. And so Job, and we, shut up. But we are not very happy with our silence. Job claims he now despises his doubt because where once he had only heard God, now he sees him, but that hardly seems satisfactory. Indeed, we feel we no longer see God, either in Behemoth or Leviathan, as God took a dip into history and finding it pretty rough made a dramatic exit.

And that makes us particularly sympathetic with Thomas and his demand to "show me." Like Thomas, especially after Auschwitz, we want to see some marks that God has not abandoned us in this mess. Auschwitz seems to be the surest sign we have that abandonment is exactly what has happened. Where is God in this? Or even more radically, if God is in this how can we possibly continue the presumption that such a god is worthy of worship? Listen to Elie Wiesel as he describes the hanging of a young boy in his classic, *Night*:

> One day when we came back from work, we saw three gallows rearing up in the assembly place, three black crows. Roll call. SS all round us, machine guns trained: the traditional ceremony. Three victims in chains—and one of them, the little servant, the sad eyed angel.
>
> The SS seemed more preoccupied, more disturbed than usual. To hang a young boy in front of thousands of spectators was no light matter. The head of the camp read the verdict. All eyes on the child. He was lividly pale, almost calm, biting his lips. The gallows threw its shadow over him.
>
> This time the Lagerkapo refused to act as executioner. Three SS replaced him.
>
> The three victims mounted together onto the chairs.
>
> The three necks were placed at the same moment within the nooses.
>
> "Long live liberty!" cried the two adults.
>
> But the child was silent.
>
> "Where is God? Where is He?" someone behind me asked.
>
> At a sign from the head of the camp, the three chairs tipped over.
>
> Total silence throughout the camp. On the horizon, the sun was setting.
>
> Bare your heads!" yelled the head of the camp. His voice was raucous. We were weeping.
>
> "Cover your heads!"
>
> Then the march past began. The two adults were no longer alive. Their tongues hung swollen, blue-tinged. But the third rope was still moving; being so light, the child was still alive . . . .

For more than half an hour he stayed there, struggling between life and death, dying in slow agony
under our eyes. And we had to look him full in the face.

He was still alive when I passed in front of him. His
tongue was still red, his eyes not yet glazed.

Behind me, I heard the same man asking:

"Where is God now?"

And I heard a voice within me answer him:

"Where is He? Here He is—He is hanging there on
this gallows . . . "

That night the soup tasted of corpses.

(pp. 75–76).

Tales about Behemoths and Leviathans do us little good
when faced by this. Nor are we sure what good it would do
to be able, like Thomas, to touch nail holes and that
wounded side.

However, it is interesting what happens when we look more
closely at our gospel text. It is a familiar text, and we feel fair-
ly sure we know how to interpret it. As I suggested, we closely identify with Thomas as we assume the issue to be one of
belief. In spite of the commendation for those who have
believed without having seen we think we might be better
believers if we could just get some better evidence. Behemoths
and Leviathans no longer witness for us a gracious creator. We
have been schooled to want to know if historically Jesus was
really about what the Gospels seem to claim. Like Thomas, we
want some good first-hand evidence.

But of course this way of understanding the text is to mis-
read it entirely. The issue was not one of belief at all — not in
Jesus or his resurrection. John was well aware that such "evi-
dence" was hardly knockdown. For example, Jesus had raised
Lazarus from the grave, but immediately after John tells us
"Many of the Jews, who had come with Mary and had seen
what he did, believed in him; but some of them went to the
Pharisees and told them what Jesus had done" (John 11:45).
Seeing is hardly believing.

What is at issue in Thomas' demand is not just evidence,
as is clear from the incompatibility of his confession with the
evidence.

For after Jesus shows him his hands and side, Thomas exclaims, "My Lord and my God!" Now that is an extraordinary deduction on the basis of the evidence. Resurrection after all does not prove lordship, but rather resurrection with the marks of crucifixion show that the resurrected Lord is not different from the crucified Lord. In John's Gospel it is in the crucifixion that we see our Lord exalted; in the resurrection we learn that our crucified Lord remains with us even now.

To know that Jesus is the Lord comes not from seeing nail holes. We are able to see the nail holes in a resurrected Lord only because, like Thomas, we have first learned to follow this Lord and thus have been trained to know how he wills to be present. Namely he is the Lord whose presence provides forgiveness and creates a community of forgiveness. For if we have received the Holy Spirit, his continuing presence, he tells us we have the power to forgive sins. And we have such power because through his cross and resurrection we know we have been forgiven. No small matter, to be sure, for it is exactly the power of God that allows us to allow ourselves to be forgiven —much more than to forgive.

Note how different this presence is than that of the incomprehensibility of the God that creates the Behemoths—what is incomprehensible is not power in and of itself, but the power that forgives. So in effect the schooling that Thomas must undergo is not unlike the schooling that we must undergo in the face of Auschwitz. Like Thomas we seek a God of power that will make the horrible reality of the Holocaust come out right, but all we find is a God whose presence and power resides in steadfast graciousness. Such a presence is easily trivialized, but when properly accepted it has a power that scares the wits out of the world. The world does not seek forgiveness but control, pretentiously assuming that it has the power to forgive.

For preaching this message of forgiveness we find Peter imprisoned. All that Peter said was, "The God of our fathers raised Jesus, whom you killed by hanging him on a tree. God exalted him at his right hand as Leader and Savior, to give repentance to Israel and forgiveness of sins. And we are witnesses to these things, and so is the Holy Spirit whom God has given to those that obey him" (Acts 5:29–32). Such preaching can also land us in prison as we find out that what we and the world want is not a God of forgiveness, but rather a God simply with power. We want a God that makes it possible to ensure "never again" when faced with Auschwitz and all we get is a God that calls us to be forgiven. For that, in short, is the heart of the Gospel—namely that we have been forgiven for the Holocaust. Resurrection is not God's retreat from us, but rather the clear sign that nothing we can do can alienate us from his steadfast will to forgive and love us and thus to make us into a people capable of forgiving and loving.

But wait a minute! This is not the message we want when faced with Auschwitz. There are at least two objections to putting the matter this way. First, many point out that there have been worse genocides in history. All this talk about the uniqueness of the Holocaust is but another way Jews are reasserting their uniqueness. And of course there is some truth to that, but indeed the Holocaust is so significant and so unique because it happened to the Jews in the midst of an ostensibly Christian civilization.

But even that fact may not cry out for our seeking forgiveness. After all we did not do it. Why do we need forgiveness for the Holocaust? We Christians in American did not do it. Indeed we fought to undo it. The attempt of many to claim responsibility for Auschwitz, or now for the evils for slavery, is but a masochistic way to secure moral identity through guilt in a morally confused civilization. And again there is some truth to that, but not very much. We simply cannot avoid, as Christians, recognizing the fact that we prepared people for the Holocaust for centuries. Who can listen, after Auschwitz, to the Johannine crucifixion account of Good Friday with its constant reference to "the Jews did this" and "the Jews did that" without feeling uncomfortable? Yet we have to go on reading those passages, since they are ours; and they must continue to remind us what havoc and evil they have wrought, culminating in the Holocaust. And by remembering we also know why we so need to be forgiven for what happened there.

An even more substantive difficulty, however, comes from the survivors of Auschwitz. For surely from their perspective Christian talk about forgiveness in connection with Auschwitz is nothing less than obscene. What gall and pretension! First the Christians kill and persecute the Jews and then they turn around and claim that God has forgiven them of such heinous crimes—not only forgiven them, but now they can learn to forgive themselves. The Jew should rightly feel that such forgiveness is surely cheap grace, but nonetheless that is what we must say. To say anything less would be to obey the world and not God and thus be robbed of the Holy Spirit we have been given through the resurrection.

Indeed Christian complicity with the Holocaust was due to our forgetting that our task was to obey God and not the way of the world. Our task was not to form a civilization where we would be safe from being thrown in jail for preaching God's forgiveness, but rather our task is to be a community of the forgiven. Such a community knows that God chooses not to rule the world by power divorced from love, but rather comes to us as the crucified Lord who remains ever ready to forgive—even the Holocaust.

I do not pretend that this message can be or should be easily accepted by Jew or Christian, but it is the message of the Gospel. Yet, I am afraid the claim is finally even more offensive than this. Indeed I hesitate to say it and certainly would try to avoid it if I were not under the discipline of these texts. For the resurrection not only means that we Christians have an obligation to accept forgiveness for the Holocaust, but we must ask the Jew to forgive us. If we do not do so we cannot help but be caught in the eternal game of "I am guiltier than you," and thus we fail to face our common destiny.

Questions of whether the Jew should be converted pale next to this message. Our task today is not to make Jews Christians, but simply to ask them to forgive us. We must do that because we believe that we worship the same God who in Christ has asked nothing new that had not already been asked of the Jew and Gentile. So we must ask Christian and Jew to see their God in each other, a God who asks of us to be open to forgiveness— with all the change of heart, mind, and behavior that forgiveness implies.

The reality of the Holocaust cannot be made to go away by continuing to weigh up guilt and responsibility. Such exercises, while not completely pointless, often come close to being obscene. Rather what we and the Jew must both do is to remember. But without forgiveness we Christians are tempted simply to forget, deny, or wallow in inaction; and Jews are tempted to lose their humanity in humiliation or vengeance. But if we are forgiven we have the chance to remember and to make this terrible event part of our common history so that we can together make a different human story for the future and look forward to the day when God's reign will come and we can embrace as brother and sister.

In the meantime, we can celebrate his presence—the presence of his Spirit among us—by learning how to allow ourselves to be forgiven and by learning what forgiveness in this case calls for. We can't very well march up to our Jewish neighbors and ask them to forgive us if we have created no other significant ties with them. With some imagination we can think of ways to let them appreciate how we—as "Easter people"—live by a new life not in triumph but in our openness to the suffering that has been theirs and is part of our history as well. In this way, we can begin a new journey together—with this week as a new beginning.

CHAPTER FIVE

Jews and Christians: All in the Family, A Sermon Based on Luke 15

William H. Willimon

> *May the God of steadfastness and encouragement enable you to live in such harmony with one another, in accord with Christ Jesus, that together you may with one voice glorify the God and Father of our Lord Jesus Christ. Welcome one another, . . . as Christ has welcomed you, for the glory of God.*

Any law enforcement officer will tell you that a policeman would rather try to stop a bank robbery than to intervene in a domestic argument. Bank robbers want only to take the money and run. But in such cases as an estranged husband or wife, two feuding brothers fighting it out in the kitchen or the bedroom—someone is likely to be hurt. More people are murdered by relatives than by strangers. Family feuds are the worst fights.

Luke tells (Luke 15) of a family feud in which an older brother and a younger brother contend with one another for their father's love. You know the story about how the younger one left home and wasted his inheritance in prodigality. When the boy returned, his father welcomed him, but not his older brother who pouted bitterly in the darkness and refused to go to his homecoming celebration. Family fights can be bitter. I have known more than one set of brothers and sisters who dishonor their dead parent's memory by refusing to speak to one another after a fight over who got the family farm.

In graduate school, when we lacked enough money to go out on a Saturday night, we would sometimes amuse ourselves by listening in on the marital disagreements of the couple who lived in the apartment next to ours. One didn't even need a glass to the wall to hear the altercations. It was harmless, cheap fun for us. Often, when we read the New Testament, we are peeking in, listening at the door, with glass put to the wall, on a family feud that has lasted centuries, a feud in which there has been little fun and much bitterness, even bloodshed—a family feud between Christian and Jew.

Today's Scripture from Romans, like much of that epistle, is part of that debate. In some of his letters, Paul pleads to his fellow Jews to accept Gentile Christians into the family of God. Here, Paul works the other side, pleading to new Gentile Christians to get along with their Jewish Christian brothers and sisters. Welcome one another, . . . as Christ has welcomed you," Paul says. To those Gentiles who put on airs and behaved haughtily toward their (probably poorer) Jewish relations, Paul says "Look, you know what it's like to be outsiders. You were outsiders, now you are insiders. You ought to welcome others in the same way that Israel has graciously welcomed you."

We, as Gentiles, are the Johnny-and-Susie-Come-Latelies to faith. We Gentiles are the eleventh-hour worker, the younger prodigal son, the foolish virgin beating on God's door, hoping that the promises given to Israel might also be given to us.

"Will the Jews be saved?" That question is sometimes asked in the church and may be of interest to us but it is of little interest to the New Testament. The question of the status of the Jews had already been answered by Scripture beginning with the promises to Abraham and Sarah, reiterated to Jacob, made manifest to Moses and the children of Israel in the Exodus, and the birth of Joshua (Jesus) at Bethlehem. God promised always to love and Scripture is the testimony to God's faithfulness. As Paul says here in Romans, "Christ became a servant to the circumcised to show God's truthfulness, in order to confirm the promises given to the patriarchs. . . ." (15:8).

Will the Jews be saved? Instead the New Testament question, the question which occupies today's epistle is: Will the *Gentiles* be saved? When God made the promise to Abraham, it was a promise to make a great nation of his descendants, not the whole world. When God stretched forth a mighty arm in the exodus from Egypt, it was to deliver Israel, not all oppressed peoples everywhere. The promises of God to save, to deliver, to love, to preserve, are promises to Israel, the Chosen People, the Light to the Nations, God's family. Will the Jews be saved? is not, according to Paul in Romans 9, 10, and 11, a question which any Bible-believing, promise trusting Christian may ask. We already know the answer. God is gracious, faithful to his promises.

The New Testament question, the debate which required massive argument and all of the theological and literary skills at Paul's disposal was, "Will the *Gentiles* be saved?" In what way is the good news of the Jew, Jesus, addressed to his fellow Jews, *our* good news? How do we stand in relation to the people who first taught us to look for a Messiah? What are we doing here today, Gentiles, reading somebody else's mail? For Paul, the ultimate wonder of Christ, the deepest marvel of the coming of Jesus, was not the virgin birth, or angels in the skies, but the gracious inclusion even of Gentiles into the promises of God to Israel. The glory of God, he says in today's Scripture, is that God has welcomed you! The father has welcomed home the younger prodigal. The door has been opened at midnight to the beseeching outsider. Those who have entered the vineyard at the close of the day are given as much as those who have trusted, believed, suffered, and been persecuted for thousands of years. God is amazingly gracious to save *even Gentiles*.

But if you have even a superficial knowledge of the history of the church's relationship to the Jews, a shudder goes down our Gentile spines. The gospel which first enabled Jews to welcome Gentiles became perverted into the separation of Gentile from Jew. By crusader's sword, Hitler's ovens, or even Christian evangelism, the once persecuted church became the persecutor of Jesus' own people. I do not have to recount for this congregation, the long, tragic story of the church's complicity and outright persecution of the Chosen People. Our infidelity, our perversion of the Gospel, transformed the cross of Christ from a symbol of salvation to the symbol of oppression and death for millions. We Christians are hurt when others say that our cross, the symbol which we honor as our hope, is a feared sign of past and potential persecution for others. It is a bitter irony that the instrument used for the torture and death of Jesus (not the first and, alas, not the last Jewish martyr) has been perverted into a sword of oppression for Jesus' kinfolk. Advent is a season of penitence, and there is much repenting for the church to do in our relationship with our brothers and sisters, the Jews.

In this sense the presence of the Jews continues to be a kind of scandal to Christians. Where Christians have become a smug, powerful majority, complacent, affluent, and secure, the Jews — the millions of victims of pogroms and concentration camps — reminds us of how painful belief in God can be. But more than that, the presence of Jews poses a stark and threatening question to us Christians: We look back upon the centuries of Christian cruelty to the Jews and wonder why our gospel failed to give more of us the resources rightly to live with, defend, and even to die for the brothers and sisters whom our Lord died to save. Under the Nazis some Christians risked their lives to help Jews. Why weren't there more Christian families, who supported their Jewish kinfolk in their time of trial?

How many Christian doors would open to a poor Jewish carpenter and his pregnant wife who had nowhere to stay during Caesar's taxation? How many of us would risk our families to save some Rachel and her Jewish boy-child from Herod's sword? This is only my theory, but I believe that one reason why there is animosity between Christian and Jew is that we Christians know, in our moments of deep honesty, how miserably our religion failed when it needed to be laid on the line for Jesus' family. We had our chance to show that faith in Jesus enables us to be courageous, peaceful, heroic, and true; and we blew it. We turned away Joseph and Mary from our door; we stopped our ears to the wailing of Rachel in Ramah.

Paul's solution to this sadness is a simple one of hospitality: *Welcome the Jew as the Jew has welcomed you.* The one who is hospitable knows what it's like to be a stranger, for he has been a stranger himself. We Gentiles have stood out in the cold. Once we were nobodies; now we are family. Let us act like it.

This does not deny that we Christians really do have differences with the Jews. The church is not the replacement for Israel. The Jews look at Jesus and do not see what we see. Rather, the Jew still asks us Christians, "If Jesus is the Redeemer, why doesn't the world look more redeemed?" It is a tough question, one which goes to the heart of our faith. To answer it we must not turn outward but inward. In particular we must not answer it in ways which forsake the religion of

Jesus—with hatred, violence, or resentment. We must answer it in the way that Jesus answered: by living lives which do not blatantly contradict the truth of which we speak.

We Gentile latecomers will not get out of our dilemma with the Jews through some sort of liberal, intellectual imperialism which demands that both Christians and Jews be converted into bland, universalized, American pagans before we can live together. Some of the silliest arguments over the future of the Duke University class ring took this point of view: Let's all agree to act less religious, suppress our distinctive beliefs and act like rational, universal human beings and then that will settle the problem of our differences. No. Religion, for Jew or Gentile, is not something we check at the door when we come to the university or walk in the voting booth. It accounts for who we are, what we want, what we are trying to be. If I am to welcome the Jew, I must welcome the Jew as a Jew, in all his or her differences and he or she must welcome me in the same way. We cannot render up our belief in Jesus as the Christ as a sort of guilt payment for our past sins against the Jews. That solves nothing.

The way for Christian and Jew to live together, is for us both to be more faithful to our beliefs. The more we Christians come to see our Christ as the fulfillment of God's promises to Israel, the more keenly we feel the unmerited quality of our amazing inclusion into those promises, the more quickly will be healed the tragic separation within the Family of God. To the extent that we Christians and Jews—allow our faith in God to be diluted through nationalistic loyalties or pagan philosophies, or other alien truth claims, we forfeit the theological resources whereby we are enabled to live together as a family. The only way I can be hospitable to any stranger is constantly to be reminded that I was a stranger, I was out in the cold, I was taken in even when I didn't deserve to be.

Luke told a story about a troubled family in which a younger son, after a lurid sojourn, returned home in rags and smelling of the cheap perfume of harlots. The waiting father received him with joy (Luke 15:1–32). A party began. But the older brother—the one who never left home, who remained in the field, faithfully working for the father—refused to go to the party. The father came out into the darkness and pleaded with the brother to come in, but to no avail.

In our day, the story has taken a sad and unexpected turn, one which Luke couldn't have imagined. The younger brother soon lost his repentant, contrite spirit. The shock of his father's gracious reception wore off. He came to resent his older brother's failure to join the party at his homecoming. He began to scheme against his brother, to take on airs, to forget how fortunate he was to be in his Father's house. At last he even resorted to locking the older brother out of the house. He bolted the door and the party which had been a celebration for the reception of a stranger, became the victory bash of the arrogant usurper.

The music and dancing resumed. The smug younger brother had it all to himself now. But outside in the December darkness stood the Father where he had left him, out in the darkness, standing where he had always been, beside the older brother.

The younger brother had succeeded in locking out his brother, he had the whole house to himself but, alas, he had locked out his loving father as well.

This sermon was delivered in the chapel of Duke University.

COMMENTARY

On "Jews and Christians: All in the Family"

Hugh Anderson

In most of the sermons in this volume, the subject of Jewish–Christian relationships can be read only between the lines, as it were. Here it is dealt with directly. The title itself leaves us in no doubt about what will be the sermon's primary subject matter.

No more does the preacher leave his hearers in any doubt about the irrefutable, tragic, and agonizing fact that across nearly two thousand years Christians have been far less than true to their own highest colors. His sermon is a powerful and very disturbing (all the better for that!) indictment of Christian prejudice, hostility, and active cruelty to Jews—from "crusader's sword" to "Hitler's ovens." It is, alas, perfectly correct to say that the cross, the supreme Christian symbol of love and hope has all too often become "a sword of oppression for Jesus' kinfolk." The course of history demonstrates how easily the highest can be perverted to the lowest.

Krister Stendahl once wrote that Christians are really "honorary Jews." The "today" of the New Testament witness to Christ could never have been without the "yesterday" of God's people, Israel, and the Hebrew Scriptures. The God whom Jesus called Father is no other than the God of Abraham, Isaac and Jacob. The fulfillment of God's purpose the early followers of Christ found in his life, death, and resurrection was the fulfillment of the promises God made of old to Israel. These early followers drew most extensively on the Old Testament, interpreting it in bold, adventurous, and imaginative ways in order to explain the nature of their experience and the ground of their faith.

All of this Willimon has brought out in his own trenchant way, and has shown how true it is that we Christians need the Jews more than they need us, since it is we who are the latecomers in God's plan of salvation. Ironically enough, we need the Jews for quite another reason, as Willimon quite justifiably claims—to keep our arrogance in check through their confronting, by their very presence, with the question of how far, as disciples of Jesus Christ, we have been instrumental in redeeming the world.

There is nothing illogical about holding that, within the wide sweep of history, we need the Jews more than they need us, and yet insisting, as Willimon properly does, that in this secular and materialist generation we do undoubtedly *need each other*. He points up how far the process of secularization has gone in Duke University—Jews and Christians in about equal proportion, but both together outnumbered—by the "nonreligious" or the "irreligious." Not mincing his words, he calls them "pagans." Quite a revelation this for one who, like myself, was a member of the Duke University Faculty in an earlier decade, when religion courses were still required of *all* students. I know this does not mean of course that *all* students back then were devoutly interested in religion.

Perhaps it would have been an impertinence to take a register of attendance in the narthex of Duke Chapel on the December morning, 1986, when this sermon was preached, but it would be interesting to know how many Jewish students, if any, were present to hear it. At all events, in an age of rampant paganism, Jews and Christians do need each other, as witnesses both, to the Beyond, the Transcendent, the one Creator and Redeemer God.

Willimon enters a very timely caveat against either side, Jews or Christians, surrendering the time honored traditions and convictions, which are the very foundation-stones of each one's existence, in favor of a bland humanism or nebulous relativism for which anything goes. The way forward is for the Jew to remain faithful to his or her Jewish beliefs, and for the Christian to remain faithful to his or hers. I have found it is very difficult indeed to persuade more conservative Christian believers that this is so. Where somewhat imperialist notions of Christian superiority tend to prevail, such believers still consider the only way ahead to be the way of mission, to bring Jews into the Christian fold.

In respect of Christian feelings of superiority, where and as they do predominate, the sermon's conclusion is a master stroke. Luke's parable of the Prodigal Son or Waiting Father is a many faceted story, but one of its intriguing features is the radical reversal of roles within it. The *wayward and rascally* younger brother turns back homeward in complete humility and contrition, asking nothing and, amid joy and celebration, is reinstated to sonship in the household by the boundless love of the Father. The dutiful elder son, taken to signify the Jew, spurns the Father's blessing and misses the celebration, in contrast to the Prodigal, taken to signify the Gentile late-comers, who come empty-handed and receive God's mercy. Willimon closes with a gripping, dramatic picture of how history has, so to speak, re-reversed these roles. The penitent younger son has become smug and arrogant, and has claimed the family household for his very own, leaving the first born, the Jew, out in the dark and cold. But the true pathos is that, in shutting out the first-born, he has also locked the door against the Father God who longed to bless his elder son.

One or two exegetical quibbles may be permitted. It is true that the question sometimes asked in the modern church, "Will the Jews be saved?" is not asked in the New Testament, certainly not in that form. But in the fervent rhetorical outburst of Romans 9, 10, and 11, Paul does ask with considerable passion: "What is to be the ultimate destiny, within the divine economy, of God's people Israel, my people, now that she has rejected Christ?" In the light of Paul's overt references to Israel's failure and stumbling in 9.30–10.4, to hold that the fate of Israel constituted no problem whatever for Paul is to over-state the case, and to discount the tension inherent in Paul's situation. To be sure, the burning question of Israel which did vex him, finds its resolution in the thought that prior advantages accrue to Israel as God's Chosen, that these are irrevocable, and that God cannot and will not forsake his people in the end. By a strange irony in the divine plan Israel's very rejection of the gospel becomes an open door for the ingathering of Gentiles, and their ingathering leads in turn to the final entry of Israel into the realm of salvation. In the metaphor of the olive tree (Israel) and the wild olive tree (the Gentiles), Paul reasserts the priority of Israel and warns against any pride on the part of the Gentiles (see the whole of chapter 11).

Willimon develops his sermon from Rom. 15.7–9:

> *Welcome one another, therefore, just as Christ has welcomed you, for the glory of God. For I tell you that Christ has become a servant of the circumcised on behalf of the truth of God in order that he might confirm the promises given to the patriarchs, and in order that the Gentiles might glorify God for his mercy.*

The internal evidence of the Letter to the Romans suggests that the community of believers in Rome, which Paul had never visited, consisted of a majority of Gentiles who had responded to the gospel and a minority of Jews who had likewise responded. The two groups in the congregation appear to be at loggerheads, though it is not easy to gather precisely what the nature of the controversy is. Much depends on how we interpret chapter 14. But the gentler tone of Romans (gentler surely than Galatians) would seem to indicate that it did not amount to open schism. What is at stake for Paul in these three verses is not quite the same as, though not unrelated to, the Jew–Gentile question as he raises it in Romans 9–11. Here in Romans 15:7–9 he is not saying that Jews as Jews had welcomed Gentiles, or requesting that Gentile outsiders, now become insiders, should welcome Jews. The preferred translation is, I think, "Accept one another as Christ has accepted you" (NEB), rather than the more usual "Welcome one another ..." (RSV)—if this is not splitting hairs. Paul is here appealing to Jews and Gentiles who are already *insiders* within the fellowship of Christ in Rome for mutual acceptance, harmony, and unity within the body corporate. He grounds his appeal on the truth of the amazing outreach of God's grace in Christ, which confers God's blessing on Jews, become believers in the gospel, in order to demonstrate his unfailing faithfulness to his promises, and on Gentiles in order that they might receive it as a glorious pledge of God's mercy and loving-kindness.

These minor exegetical observations must not be allowed to detract from the potent impact of a sermon which, in its balanced admixture of realism and idealism, is an eloquent and inspiring contribution toward better mutual understanding between Jew and Christian today. By the same token there is here no compromising of the distinctiveness of either Judaism or Christianity for the sake of a cozy togetherness.

CONCLUSION

The Agenda for Preachers and Teachers

Joseph Stoutzenberger

The essays collected in this volume address the question, "Can the Good News as preached in Christian churches be good news for Jews as well?" Two presumptions underlie this question. First, Christian preaching from apostolic times to the present frequently built its case on bad news for Jews. Secondly, Christian preaching today must on the one hand actively counteract anti-Judaism found in Scripture or tradition and on the other hand advocate a new vision of the relationship between Christianity and Jews and Judaism.

The essays brought together here address the dilemma that preaching on certain biblical texts in a simplistic or insensitive can lead to very unbiblical attitudes toward Jews and Judaism. Preaching on these difficult texts, to use Clark Williamson's term, requires knowledge of contemporary biblical scholarship, awareness of the contexts in which such texts are set, recognition that specific passages must be viewed in light of broader scriptural themes, and consciousness of the legacy of anti-Judaism that has helped shape the person-in-the-pew's understanding of the Christian message over against Judaism. Christian preaching today must include both renunciation of past misconceptions and annunciation of a new, more authentic appreciation of Judaism. Silence on the issue is not an option; in the past silence by Christians has proved deadly to Jews.

As the essays make clear, preaching that is sensitive to Jews may at times appear to be stealing the thunder from important Scripture passages.

For example:

— Isn't "Pharisee" simply a code word for hypocrite? In our preaching mustn't we condemn hypocrisy/"Phariseeism" even though for many in the congregation the terms are associated with Jews of Jesus' day? We must understand that the major aim of the Pharisees was to discover and live by the relevance of the Jewish tradition for them and their contemporaries, gathered in prayerful study of the Scriptures.

— Do we need to interrupt the drama of Holy Week's passion play with an asterisk explaining that the crowd screaming "Crucify him!" does not refer to "the Jews" as a whole as the text implies? The essays gathered here insist that much of the old, time-honored symbol system must be replaced with new renderings of the relationship between early Christianity and Judaism. And, in fact, the "new" symbol system more accurately portrays the state of affairs in first century Judaism out of which Christianity emerged.

The preceding essays, therefore, show that this new preaching can enliven the Christian message and does not reduce it to bland, politically correct piety. It can challenge anew the Christian community and more accurately represent the message of Jesus. A collage of essays, each one addresses the topic from the point of view of its author. Both Protestant and Catholic scholars are represented. The initial seven essays in Section One speak about preaching while the remaining four in Section Two represent actual sermons preached.

Martin Marty focuses effectively on the broad issue, drawing on his impressive scholarly background as historian, but also on his continuing involvement in the moral and religious dimensions of contemporary issues. A penetrating and perceptive survey of what has happened to foster Christian–Jewish mutual understanding is offered by John T. Pawlikowski in "Accomplishments and Challenges in the Jewish–Christian Encounter." He surveys changes in historical, biblical, and theological perceptions in the past thirty years which have put in a new light the origins of Jewish–Christian differences.

Clark Williamson and Ronald J. Allen begin their contribution to this conversation on a negative note, reminding their readers that certain anti-Jewish themes are "simply part of the furniture of the church in which those who become preachers are socialized." In all likelihood the four anti-Jewish themes that they describe will sound familiar to Christians who preach or hear sermons. They propose "alternative hermeneutical and homiletical moves" that will prove helpful to preachers who want to rearrange "the furniture"—their approach to anti-Jewish themes embedded in the Scriptures as described.

In his essay Harry Cargas makes a plea for repentance by Christians concerning the Holocaust, beginning by acknowledging the stark reality that "probably every killer of Jews in the Shoah—every single murderer—was a baptized Christian." (1) Cargas moves on to encourage preachers to avoid being "post-Holocaust accomplices" (2) in the way they preach about Jews and Judaism.

David Read's "Reflections" journeys into that territory where autobiography and history meet. While he is unashamedly autobiographical, he proposes that his story mirrors that of many Christian preachers, especially those in the Calvinist tradition. In this way he identifies attitudes toward contemporary Jews not uncommon among preachers trained in the thirties, forties, and fifties: "Crudely speaking, we were left with the impression that the Jews were a wonderful people who 'missed the boat' when Jesus came. From the evangelical point of view, they should be targeted for conversion; from the liberal, they were seen as 'near Christian' with Unitarian convictions." Dr. Read cautions preachers today to demonstrate increased respect for contemporary Jews by rejecting silence on controversial issues, by examining assumptions and misrepresentations about Jews and Judaism that may slip into their preaching, and finally by engaging in dialogue with Jews.

Robert Daly, S.J., offers practical tips about how preachers can deal with specific Scripture passages that may strike hearers as anti-Jewish. His four "how to" suggestions provide the type of clear-cut guidelines by which preachers will want to scrutinize their own homiletic approach to Scripture.

Peter Phan moves the discussion specifically into the Catholic arena. His starting point is not Scripture but the recently promulgated *Catechism* of the Catholic Church. His contention, that the *Catechism* will be the shaping document for Catholic preaching for years to come, has yet to be proven. Nonetheless, it is valuable for Catholics and other Christians concerned about the current state of Jewish–Christian relations to situate the *Catechism* in the tradition of official church documents beginning with Vatican II's *Nostra Aetate*. Phan finds both development and regression in the *Catechism*'s contribution to the topic. His essay gives a thorough overview of how the document approaches Judaism and the Jewish–Christian relationship.

In section II of this book are sermons which seek to demonstrate how one should go about "removing anti-Judaism from the pulpit."

Carol Ann Morrow's contribution chronicles strategies used by two Xavier University professors to assist Christians in coming to grips with anti-Judaism in Christian Scriptures and traditions. In so far as preaching also involves teaching, approaches illustrated by Morrow can effectively carry over to the pulpit.

The remaining sermons highlight the theme of Jewish–Christian relations. Individually they may appeal more to the heart or to the head; the focus may be on Scripture or on current events. Nonetheless, each one demonstrates how a sermon can incorporate the theme of Christian relations with Jews and Judaism so as to present the Good News in authentic, challenging, and sensitive ways.

Nancy Malone's sermon becomes a meditation on the rich but ambiguous symbolism of the cross. So central a symbol for Christians, historically the cross has too often been associated with domination and persecution for Jews. Malone entreats her hearers to take up the cross but as rooted in its more prototypically Christian sense, as a symbol of resistance to oppression.

In his sermon Wallace Alston uses Rom. 11:18 to attack anti-Judaism head on. He emphasizes the often forgotten truth of Christian indebtedness to Judaism. Culminating his sermon on a practical note, Alston offers three pointers about where Christians should be today in their relations with Jews.

In Stanley Hauerwas' sermon for Eastertime he links resurrection with forgiveness, rather than power and control, and explores how openness to forgiveness is the appropriate stance Christians today should have toward Jews. Given the history of Christian–Jewish relations, contemplating the creative power of forgiveness is an appropriate starting point for transforming Christian preaching on Judaism.

The last contribution by Will Willimon is a slightly revised version of a sermon delivered in 1985 at Duke University. He makes creative use of the two sons in the parable of the Prodigal Son to illustrate how relations between Christians and Jews have turned topsy-turvy, distorting the original message of the parable. Willimon finds that the presence of Jews poses a threatening question to Christians: "We look back upon the centuries of Christian cruelty to Jews and wonder why our gospel failed to give more of us the resources rightly to live with, defend, and even to die for the brothers and sisters whom our Lord died to save."

This compendium of essays and sermons is not meant to be the final word on the subject. Hopefully the reader will be drawn to learn more about recent studies that shed light on first-century Jewish and Christian communities along with the conflicts, social movements, and theological developments therein. Also, Christian readers might seek opportunities to engage in interreligious dialogue with Jews in order to stay current with actual concerns that exist in the communities where they live and preach.

Finally, the goal of the book has been met if Christian preachers conscientiously take steps to make their preaching of the Good News good news for Jews as well.

INDEX

Removing Anti-Judaism From the Pulpit

Sixth in a Series by the
American Interfaith Institute
and
World Alliance of Interfaith Organizations

Also published by the American Interfaith Institute and Continuum

The Dead Sea Scrolls: Rule of the Community
Edited by James H. Charlesworth

This edition of the Rule of the Community is published in cooperation with the American Interfaith Institute and the Israel Museum's Shrine of the Book. The book incorporates state of the art photography and transcription of the original Hebrew text. To make the Scroll accessible to the world community, this edition includes translations in English, Spanish, French, Italian, German, and modern Hebrew.

Also published by Continuum

Jewish Perspectives on Christianity:
Leo Baeck, Martin Buber, Franz Rosenzweig, Will Herberg,
Abraham J. Heschel
Edited by Fritz A. Rothschild

"The theological causes and implications of the fateful split between Judaism and Christianity is a topic of perennial interest to thinkers of both faiths. This anthology . . . brings together substantial excerpts from the works of five leading Jewish thinkers of the twentieth century. Introductions to these thinkers have been contributed by five currently active Christian scholars. This interreligious dimension enhances the book's potential to advance Jewish–Christian dialogue. . . . Strongly recommended."
—*Choice*